C50 1505374 3E

£17.99

AUTHOR

Public Relations

WITHDRAWN

BOOKS IN THE SERIES

The Practice
of
Public Relations

Fourth Edition

Edited by

Sam Black, MBE, Hon FIPR, FIMgt, FRSA
Honorary Professor of Public Relations, University of Stirling

Butterworth-Heinemann Ltd
Linacre House, Jordan Hill, Oxford OX2 8DP

℞ A member of the Reed Elsevier plc group

OXFORD   LONDON   BOSTON
MUNICH   NEW DELHI   SINGAPORE   SYDNEY
TOKYO   TORONTO   WELLINGTON

First published 1982
Second edition 1985
Reprinted 1985
Third edition 1988
Reprinted 1989, 1990, 1992, 1994
Fourth edition 1995

British Library Cataloguing in Publication Data
Practice of Public Relations. – 4Rev.ed. –
(Marketing Series: Professional
Development)
I. Black, Sam II. Series
659.20941

ISBN 0 7506 2318 7

Printed and bound in Great Britain by
Clays Ltd, St Ives plc

Contents

DTI financial assistance scheme, the case study of IAC Ltd, the correct use of words, the Plain English campaign, the Crystal Mark, house journals and newsletters, a new reference database, the powerful effect of images, symbolism, increasing sophistication of design, the effective use of photography, the impact of CD-ROM, 'virtual reality', the ethical implications of new technology.

Illustrations

Contributors

Sam Black, MBE, HON FIPR, HON FNIPR, FIMGT, FRSA has played a significant role in the development of both the Institute of Public Relations (IPR) and the International Public Relations Association (IPRA) since their inception in 1948 and 1955 respectively. During his career he has specialized in the trade association field and in the organization of conferences and exhibitions worldwide. Since 1975 he has concentrated on the development of public relations education at the graduate and undergraduate levels. In September 1980 he organized the special IPRA Educators' Meeting in Hong Kong, which led to the publication of IPRA Gold Paper No 4–*A Model for Public Relations Education for Professional Practice*. Sam Black used this Gold Paper effectively in the United Kingdom to convince the University of Stirling of the desirability of introducing a master's degree in public relations. This successful course, which started in 1988, has been followed by many other degree programmes in the UK. Since 1990 he has been Honorary Professor of Public Relations at the University of Stirling and he has received similar acknowledgement at other universities in the UK, Spain and China. His recent books include: *The Essentials of Public Relations*, *International Public Relations Case Studies*, *Introduction to Public Relations*, and *Exhibitions and Conferences from A to Z*.

John Cole-Morgan, BSC (AGRIC), DIP CAM, FIPR, graduated in agriculture from the University of Reading in 1960 and after a year as a farm manager joined the Public Relations Department of the Animal Foods Division of Spillers Ltd, specializing in agricultural public relations; he subsequently worked for the Agricultural Engineers Association, Astral Public Relations as agricultural account manager and Fisons before entering government service as Head of Information of the Agricultural Research Council in 1971. In 1975 he went to the Department of Trade as Head of Publicity for the British Overseas Trade Board and in 1979 became Deputy Head of the Department. From 1981 to 1984 he was Director of Public Relations to the British Council. In 1984 he became an independent public relations consultant specializing in Dorset affairs. He has been a member of the IPR Council, Chairman of its International Committee and Chairman of its Education Committee.

Betty Dean, BA, PCGE, DIPCAM, MAIE DIP, CIM DIP, MIPR is Course Director of the Watford/PRCA Diploma in International Public Relations at the Watford School of Business, West Herts College, Watford. Before training as a lecturer at Garnett College in 1984, she worked in publishing, at UIT (a branch of the United Nations in Geneva) and in industry. She was Group Public Relations Officer for a British multinational company, Unicorn Industries Ltd, in the 1970s and then became Marketing Manager for an American company operating in the acoustics business, before moving into education and creating the Watford/PRCA Diploma in International Public Relations programme. Apart from this experience, Betty Dean has been a judge for the IPR Sword of Excellence, an examiner for the BAIE Diploma and a judge for the HEIST Awards. She is a Board Member of CERP Education and is past Co-convenor of PREF (the Public Relations Educators Forum). Betty Dean is a Visiting Professor at ISERP, France, and adjunct Professor, International Public Relations, University of Syracuse (London Centre).

Rosemary Graham, BA, MSC, MIPR, MIPRA is a highly successful public affairs manager with extensive experience in both the public and private sectors and is currently Public Policy and Communication Manager with the Royal Automobile Club and has been a regular contributor to radio and television programmes on many aspects of motoring and transport policy. She started her career in financial management with Ferranti Ltd, moved into general management and then went to public affairs in the National Health Service and the university field. A two-year secondment to Whitehall followed as a Senior Principal in a major policy unit. Rosemary Graham has had both in-house experience and consulting experience of public affairs management. She took the full-time masters public relations course at the University of Stirling and was awarded the MSc.

Mark D Grundy, BA (HONS), (CANTAB), read law at Queen's College, Cambridge, graduating in 1960. He was articled to a Lincoln's Inn Fields firm of Solicitors, Messrs Rooper & Whateley, and qualified in 1963, becoming a salaried partner in the firm in 1967. In 1970 the firm merged with the larger firm of Lee & Pembertons in Gray's Inn and has remained so ever since. In 1967 he set up through his firm the Legal Advice Service for the members of the Institute of Public Relations, which has continued for the past twenty-seven years, and he has been Legal Adviser to the IPR throughout this period. He is also Legal Adviser to the Public Relations Consultants Association and runs a Legal Advice service for its consultancy members through the firm of Lee & Pembertons, where, now one of the senior partners, he has specialized in private company and commercial work and latterly in private client work, including charities and non-profit-making organizations.

Jane Hammond, DIPCAM, FIPR, is an independent public relations consultant and trainer with her own consultancies: Trident Public Relations, which she acquired in 1980, and Trident Training Services, which she set up in 1988. She has had practical experience of working both in large and small organizations, commercial and non-commercial, and as a public relations consultant specializing in small businesses and charities. She was in charge of public relations for St Teresa's Hospital and the Community Relations Commission (now the Commission for Racial Equality) and also held in-house public relations positions with the BBC, Swissair, NALGO (now Unison) and Hammersmith Council. For two years she was editor of Hollis Public Relations, and was assistant editor of the trade monthly *Dairy Industries* and health service reporter for NALGO's monthly newspaper, *Public Service*. Since 1984 she has run public relations courses leading to the CAM Certificate and Diploma. She is a tutor for the Distance Learning Diploma Programme run by the Public Relations Education Trust. She also runs her own training courses for clients, which have included the European Foundation, the Gulf Cooperation Council and the British Council (for the Soros Foundation in Romania).

Brian Harvey, BA, MIPR, FRSA, was appointed Head of Customer and Media Relations for Knowsley Metropolitan Borough Council in 1990. Before that he worked as Head of Marketing and Promotion for the Merseyside Tourist Board. He started his career as a personnel officer with ICI Ltd and then followed a total of twelve years working as a presenter and producer in local radio, for both the BBC and independent stations. He is the winner of a Rediffusion Award for Best Education Programme, two of his programmes won Gold Medals in the International Radio Festival at New York, and he was also nominated for a Sony Award in the Best Local Radio Programme category. Between 1990 and 1993 he was a member of the North West Consultative Council of the Independent Television Commission and for three years has served on the Management Committee of the Local Government Group of the Institute of Public Relations. He was the winner of an Excellence in Communication Award in 1991. Among his outside interests are the arts in Merseyside: for five years he was a director of the Liverpool Playhouse Theatre and is a long-serving trustee of the Liverpool Festival of Comedy.

Danny Moss, BA, MA, MIPR, MCIM, is a Senior Fellow at The Manchester Metropolitan University, where he is responsible for leading the University's Masters Degree in Public Relations. Before taking up his present post, Danny Moss spent some six years at the University of Stirling, where he held the position of Director of Public Relations Programmes. While at Stirling he was responsible for the introduction of the first dedicated Masters Degree in Public Relations in the United Kingdom and for the subsequent development of the first distance-learning Master's programme in public relations. Danny Moss is a founding member of the Public Relations Educators' Forum (PREF) and has delivered a number of papers on various aspects of public relations, including papers at the Public Relations World Congress (1987), and the European Confederation of Public Relations Annual Conference: (1990 and 1991). He is also a Visiting Professor at the University of Orebro in Sweden. In addition to writing and editing much of Stirling's distance learning material, Danny Moss is the author of *Public Relations in Practice: A Casebook*, and is currently working on two further books for the publishers Routledge.

Margaret Nally, HON FIPR, DIP PR (CAM), HON CERP, was born in Essex. She followed three examination courses in her last two years at the local grammar school. She left a protected job to join WRNS as Fleet Air Arm radio mechanic. In 1955, with three children and business and local journalistic experience, she moved to London to join national journalism or public relations. Two years later, established in the latter, she joined the IPR, she served on the Council and committees, including chair of Education, at establishment of CAM. She has been a solo independent consultant since 1965, dealing with a range of business and industrial clients. Elected fellow of IPR in 1972, she was the first woman President, 1976. She held offices with CERP (European Confederation of Public Relations) from 1976, and was made an Honorary Member in 1989. She was the editor, 1991, of *International Public Relations in Practice*. Her writing, lecturing and work with international interests and education continues.

Phyllis Oberman, MCAM, FIPR, has worked in public relations for thirty years. She has served three terms on the Council of the Institute of Public Relations and also on its International Committee. She has represented the IPR on the Council and Executive Committee of the European Public

Relations Confederation. She is a member of the Association of Women in Public Relations and the Writers Guild, and has co-authored four books – one cookbook and three on home interest subjects. Her wide-ranging public relations career has included positions both in-house and with consultancies. During her seventeen years as Head of Public Relations with T1 Domestic Appliances she pioneered the creation of, and took responsibility for, a consumer relations section. As a consultant and director with Paragon Communications for six years, she handled many well-known accounts in the consumer field. At this time she served on the Consumer Standards Advisory Committee of the British Standards Institution. For over four years she was Public Affairs Adviser to the Chairman of Yale and Valor and advised the management on corporate affairs as well as liaising with the firm's financial public relations consultants. She currently runs her own consultancy, with clients in consumer products and services, interior design and charities, as well as acting as a senior consultant with several public relations agencies. Phyllis Oberman is a Public Relations Consultants Association Independent Registered Consultant.

Michael Regester, FIPR, MIPRA, is joint managing director of the London-based public relations consultancy Regester and Larkin Ltd. He is widely regarded as having pioneered many of the procedures that companies can implement to prepare themselves to cope with the worst of all possible circumstances. He advises companies around the world on communications strategy when they are faced with a serious corporate crisis, and is a frequent lecturer on the subject to students at Cambridge and other universities. He is the author of *Crisis Management*, published by Business Books Ltd in 1987, and co-author of *Investor Relations*, published by Business Books Ltd in 1990.

Douglas Smith, BA (HONS), MCAM, FIPR, has been active in public relations consultancy for more than thirty years, recently as a specialist in UK and government affairs. On leaving London University he worked briefly for the *Daily Mirror* before joining the publicity staff of the Conservative Central Office in 1960. He was an adviser to Sir Edward Heath during Britain's negotiations to enter the European Community in 1962–3, following which he went into general consultancy with Planned Public Relations and other companies. He founded his own London consultancy in 1976, now part of the International Communications Group, but remains Chairman of PMS Ltd, a major UK political monitoring company, and Chief Executive of Westminster Advisers Ltd. He was for twenty-five years a local councillor in London, holding several senior chairmanships – Chairman of the Public Relations Consultants Association (1984–5), President of the Institute of

Public Relations 1990, and President CERP (European Public Relations Confederation) Consultants 1992–4. He is currently a CERP main board member.

Tim Traverse-Healy, OBE, HON FIPR, FIPA, DIPCAM, FRSA, has had a very distinguished career as a public relations consultant and educator. He has advised numerous International and European corporations and institutions on aspects of their corporate affairs activities. From 1952 to 1992 he was Public Affairs Adviser to National Westminster Bank. In 1994, he was appointed Professor of Public Relations at the University of Stirling. He has been a Visiting Professor at Baylor University, Texas, since 1988 and Honorary Professor at the University of Wales since 1990. He has been a guest lecturer at many business schools, including Harvard, London, Manchester, Henley, Cranfield, Ashridge, Templeton, INSEAD and IMEDE, and at many universities, including Warwick, Nottingham, Aston, Stirling, Wales, the Sorbonne, Boston, San Diego, Cairo, Beirut, Jerusalem, Rome, Oslo, Bruges and Ulster. Traverse-Healy has made a significant contribution to the development of Public Relations through his presidency of the Institute of Public Relations, the International Public Relations Association and the International Public Relations and Research and Education Foundation. He was Chairman of the Public Relations Education Trust (PRET) from 1990 to 1992 and a Vice-President of the European Public Relations Confederation (CERP). He served in the Royal Marine Commandos and Special Forces from 1941 to 1946. From 1947 to 1993 he was senior partner of Traverse-Healy Ltd.

Neville Wade, DIP PR (CAM), FCAM, FIPR, is an independent consultant specializing in strategic corporate communication management. His public relations career started in 1963 in local government and was followed by fifteen years working in-house for two manufacturers of capital equipment. In 1979 he established a small marketing communication consultancy in Winchester that concentrated on services for business-to-business clients. Then in 1985 he joined Welbeck Golin/Harris Communications Limited as a main board director, where he stayed for six years. Since 1974 he has served on the Council and various committees of The Institute of Public Relations and was President in 1982. Chairmanships include the Education, Professional Practices and Disciplinary committees of the IPR, as well as its Home Counties North Regional Group. He has served as a trustee on the Public Relations Education Trust and has completed two three-year sessions as a chief examiner for the CAM Diploma in Public Relations. He has also served on the executive board of the Public Relations Consultants Association and chaired its Education and Training Committee. He was the first recipient of the IPR CAM Diploma award and received the CAM Vice-Chairman's award as the first person to achieve distinctions in all examination papers.

Sue Wolstenholme, MIPR, MIPRA, has been the subject group leader at the College of St Mark and St John, Plymouth, since 1990. The college, whose degrees are validated by Exeter University, was one of the first to introduce a UK undergraduate public relations programme in 1989. Since then the number of public relations students at the college has risen from 20 to 200. In addition to their BA Honours degree, they can study with colleagues from France, Belgium, Germany, Portugal and The Netherlands for the Master of Arts degree in European Public Relations, which is jointly validated by Exeter University and the Sorbonne. Sue is European director of the MA course, leads the BA course at the College and works as a partner in the consultancy Coleridge Public Relations.

Preface to the fourth edition

This book was designed, in the first instance, for the guidance of Communication, Advertising and Marketing Education Foundation (CAM) students and to cover broadly the subject matter with which CAM Certificate students are expected to be familiar. It is equally relevant, however, for all students of public relations in undergraduate programmes in public relations or business studies.

The theory of public relations does not change but the practice develops with the new ideas and methods of management and business. The authors are very experienced in the different fields about which they have written and I would like to thank them for their willingness to share their knowledge with readers.

Acknowledgement is due to the Institute of Public Relations for permission to publish the IPR Code of Professional Conduct and its interpretation, and to the CAM Foundation for its encouragement and assistance.

I hope this new updated fourth edition will prove as popular with students as the previous editions edited by Wilfred Howard.

S B

Introduction

Sam Black

The practice of public relations in the United Kingdom has roots stretching back into the nineteenth century but its modern development as a management discipline can be dated more accurately to 1948, when the Institute of Public Relations (IPR) was formed in London.

Many men and women had carried out public relations programmes before the Second World War and then in the services and were keen to develop this experience in civilian life. Public relations was well-established in local government, and senior members of the National Association of Local Government Officers (NALGO) were prominent in the negotiations that led to the formation of the new Institute on 10 February 1948. The story of how a handful of men and women forming the IPR in 1948 has led to an active body with over 5000 members is a measure of the way in which public relations practice has become accepted as a valuable element of business practice in all fields, political, commercial and non-commercial.

This book has played a valuable part in guiding students and newcomers to the field to a thorough understanding of the principles of public relations and the ways in which they can be used to develop successful public relations programmes. The book first appeared in 1982, edited by Wilfred Howard, a distinguished public relations practitioner and a past president of the Institute of Public Relations. Under his guidance several new editions were produced, and the objective of this new fourth edition, under a new editor, is to continue the tradition that has been established and to introduce some new authors, who describe the latest theories and practice and new techniques.

The IPR definition is perhaps the most useful one for our purpose. It states:

Public relations practice is the planned and sustained effort to establish and maintain goodwill and mutual understanding between an organization and its publics.

This book seeks to translate this general statement into practical ways in which the discipline can contribute to efficiency and success in many different fields.

The IPR definition stresses very important elements of our work. It must be *planned*, it must be *sustained*, and its main thrust is aimed at establishing and maintaining *goodwill and mutual understanding*. These are aspirations to which all fair-minded people would subscribe, but how to achieve these desirable goals requires a thorough familiarity with the principles of public relations and sound experience in translating theories into successful practice.

Used correctly, public relations does not restrict its role to interpreting its organization to its publics but also endeavours to keep its management informed about their expectations. This is the essence of achieving the two-way mutual understanding emphasized in the IPR definition. There are many factors, both internal and external, which affect an organization's reputation and credibility, and these require careful study and evaluation before definitive public relations programmes can be formulated.

Public relations may be reactive or proactive. Reacting to a sudden emergency or countering adverse criticism may require immediate action. Under normal circumstances, however, public relations is not a 'fire brigade' response but should be an integral part of corporate strategy and forward planning.

In normal conditions there will usually be four stages in planning:

1 Research and analysis.
2 Planning and budgeting.
3 Carrying out the approved programme.
4 Monitoring and evaluation.

These four stages are self-explanatory and are not only relevant to public relations practice but are equally true of other aspects of management. The initial research may be fairly straightforward but may require commissioned opinion or market research. Before setting out to modify attitudes or opinions, it is obviously important to establish the current state of reputation, credibility and confidence.

The planning stage should establish priorities and time scales because these will have a profound effect on the success of the programme. Timing is particularly important and may make the difference between success and failure.

The final stage is often overlooked or restricted by an inclination to proceed with the next problem or challenge. This temptation should be resisted, because the successful operation of a programme requires careful monitoring and possible amendment or variation in the time scale.

Evaluation or measurement of results will provide valuable data for future programmes, and managements are becoming increasingly keen to have quantitative results for the financial and staff resources involved.

Towards specialization?

With the increasing complexity of business life there is a move towards specialization and some practitioners prefer to concentrate on comparatively small sectors of public relations practice. This tendency is reflected in the institute forming vocational and special interest groups catering for members with leanings towards certain fields. These special groups cover 'government affairs', 'city and financial', 'local government', 'fifth estate', 'construction', 'health and medical', 'psychology', 'technology and engineering', and 'tourism and leisure'.

This development reinforces the view that public relations practice mirrors medical practice. Those wishing to enter the medical profession first study for a general medical degree. They are then free to decide if they wish to enter general practice or to specialize as surgeons or to devote their main efforts towards some other niche in the whole medical spectrum. Similarly, a man or woman deciding to study public relations has plenty of time to decide if they wish to work in the corporate field, or the charity world or any of the many other alternatives. Some may wish to acquire public relations skills to use in quite different activities. There is no doubt that a good understanding of public relations can be a positive asset in many different walks of life.

Duties and responsibilities

The corporate structure of any large organization is usually a combination of past history and the personal choices of top management. The demand that the head of public relations in a company should be automatically a member of the board is, in my opinion, ill-conceived. This concept is unlikely to have general application, nor is it always desirable, as membership of the board is likely to lead to responsibilities that may dilute the public relations role.

A more positive approach is to emphasize the need for the head of public relations to have easy and speedy access to the chairman or chief executive officer (CEO).

Public relations must be the responsibility of the decision-maker but it can only achieve its full impact if top management fully appreciate the importance of this activity in business. Sir John Harvey-Jones, an accepted management expert, stated in *The Economist* that the main activities with which a company chairman should concern himself are strategic planning and public relations. This is undoubtedly true, but in practice, if control of overall policy is retained, operational control has to be delegated.

The question of status will depend to a certain extent on whether an organization has a large in-house department or uses outside public relations consultants, or there is a combination of the two. This is considered in depth in Chapter 10.

A trade or profession?

There is often argument as to whether public relations practitioners are carrying out a profession or a trade. This is rather a futile argument as it begs the really important question. 'What is the attitude of practitioners and how do they behave in their work?' Early in its existence the Institute of Public Relations realized the importance of ethical standards and professional competence, and since 1963 all members have had to abide by the strict conditions of the IPR Code of Professional Conduct. Business ethics has rightly become a matter of public concern and this important subject is dealt with in Chapter 11, which includes the full text of the IPR Code of Professional Conduct.

Familiarity breeds favourability

Professor Bob Worcester, chairman of Market Opinion & Research International (MORI), has used opinion research and market research very effectively to explain some of the theories of public relations that are difficult to quantify. In a lecture at Templeton College, Oxford, Worcester emphasized that in his work he had found consistently that 'Familiarity breeds favourability, not contempt'. He went on:

> Nine times out of ten, the better known a company is, the better regarded. This is true of the general public... Companies get to be well known, most of them, anyway, by doing good things to people, and by doing so, gain esteem. This in turn aids their recruitment and retention of staff, share purchase and its retention, the ear of the editor and journalist, consideration by the customer and potential customer, reflection by the politician and senior civil servant. There are a few companies that have tried to fight against this, not many successfully.

What of the future?

Since public relations is a function of management, its future role will be determined by the way in which businesses will develop. In this connection it is useful to consider the report on 'Tomorrow's Company' by the Royal Society of Arts' special working party, which has been studying this question.

In its interim report, it stressed that the successful company will be one that conforms to the following principles:

1 It will be clear about its own distinctive purpose and values.
2 It will give a lead in all its relationships by communicating its purpose and values in a consistent manner.
3 It will recognize that all its relationships are reciprocal.
4 It will see itself as part of a wider system.
5 It will recognize the potential need to make trade-offs between stakeholders.
6 It will recognize the need to measure and communicate its performance in all its relationships.

These maxims illustrate the growing perception that the reputation of a company as a good corporate citizen makes a crucial competitive difference. Or, to put it another way, 'public relations is an essential element in effective and successful business today'.

The many different ways in which public relations can contribute to the achievement of objectives and the successful and harmonious operation of an organization will be examined systematically in the following chapters.

1

Public relations in Action

Tim Traverse-Healy

Before considering the way in which public relations operates, it is logical to consider the reasons why this management discipline has increased in importance under existing conditions in the political, commercial and non-commercial fields.

After discussing the rationale and methodology of public relations in this chapter, the techniques and skills used to meet specific needs and challenges will be explored in detail by other practitioners with special experience in the particular field.

Four political, social and cultural forces have been at work over the past fifty years shaping the role and the task of the public relations practitioner. These are:

1   The information debate.
2   The interdependence factor.
3   The balance philosophy.
4   Individualism.

The information debate

The information debate has raged since the early 1950s, fuelled by the demands of the returning service men and women, changes in educational systems in Europe, the campaigning of pressure and specific interest groups, the opportunism of political parties and individual politicians. Governments and national and international major institutions and corporations have had to respond.

The cry used to be 'Information is Power'. It then became 'to lack information is to be deprived' and later 'to withhold information is an infringement of personal, civil or even human rights'. The debate moved on and continues around the twin themes 'if a right to information exists then a right to communicate or respond also exists'. Furthermore, 'if people have the right to information and to communicate and respond, then they should be given the resources to respond in equal measure'.

On the international front – the United Nations and the EU – and at national levels laws now grant rights to the public and specifically to shareholders, employers, customers, legislators and administrators. These cover such items as an institution's plans and performance, financial results, job security, products and services and social impact. Laws and regulations increasingly determine not only what information must be released and when, but even the form and language in which it must be promulgated, spanning such activities as financial reports, corporate news releases, corporate print, advertising, speeches and statements and employee communication.

These changes have created a new dictionary of terms: transparency, visibility, accountability, disclosure, governance. This popular movement has meant that the task of amassing information has become more costly and time-consuming and the arranging of its release more complex. Hence the need for maximum professionalism in the information and communication field in which the 'communication explosion' is occurring.

The interdependence factor

In the 1950s and early 1960s most citizens in Europe wanted to live in a stable society in peace and prosperity. Increasingly, however, leaders in the community came to recognize that a stable society is not necessarily a static one. Moreover, in the same period vast changes of a social, political, technical, cultural and even moral nature were taking place. None could be considered in isolation, since they were interrelated. Conflicts arose as individual societies and their sub-systems were reduced, expectations were not met and disillusionment grew.

Since the late 1960s, however, a compensating belief has emerged, one based on the reality of unity. Recognition of the 'interdependence factor' as the amalgam that binds together persons, communities, nations and continents has taken hold. So has the need for institutions to consider the social impact of their decisions and activities, often a complex and professional task.

The balance philosophy

For many years business has become concerned as to whether or not the corporation as it is presently manifested will survive into the next century. If ten years ago you asked a company chairman what his objectives were, he would probably have answered 'to make a profit and to give a good return to the owners, the shareholders'. The chances are that today the modern breed of CEOs, would say cryptically, that they wanted 'to survive', or, more expansively, 'to provide a return to the shareholders, security and a future for the employees and a good product at a fair price to customers'. If prompted, some might go on to add 'to grow, to be sensitive of our community, to be a good citizen, to be socially responsible'.

The point is that in a climate of opinion wherein interdependence is recognized as a factor it is becoming increasingly accepted by modern management that its prime task is to attempt to balance the drive for profits and commercial success against corporate concern for public policies.

The pursuit of profits will not cease but it is becoming better understood that this cannot be the only objective and profits will only be attained when the organization has an acceptable public policy. Helping managers to achieve this balance is the type of task for which the experienced public relations practitioner is well fitted. Almost by definition there is almost always a conflict of interest between the various stakeholders in an enterprise. Being seen to be sensitive to that fact and endeavouring to resolve such conflicts are part of the public relations objectives.

Individualism

Forecasters differ as to what the next century will bring, but they all seem to agree that there will be a massive shift towards public concern with human values. The signs are that the focus of power is swinging away from institutions towards individuals, especially those who can use information technology and communication and can create networks to influence action. It is generally accepted today that the general public is a mythical concept. The public is made up of a series of overlapping, interlocking minorities incorporating individuals, together making up the fabric of our society.

Providing for the needs, addressing the expectations, and matching the values of these individuals is increasingly the challenge facing institutions of all sizes. Continuing to respond by mass communication alone, unrelated to information, education, participation and dialogue, will prove a snare and a delusion. Public relations practitioners, with their understanding of interactive communication and the impact of technology in this regard, will be ideally placed to aid managements to meet the challenges of the new conditions.

The methodology of public relations

The practice of public relations employs some or all of a large battery of 'tools'. With one exception, broadcasting, they have not been added to over the years. Moreover, as new techniques become available or popular, they do not push out existing practices.

The list is a long one: speeches, statements, position papers, reports, research, briefings, seminars, conferences, interviews, professional contacts, networking, community service, advertising, direct mail, broadcasting, editorial and print. It is important to realize that singly or plurally none of this long list constitutes public relations.

Public relations is why, when, where and how you use it. The temptation – even the pressures – to jump directly into action and to become 'technique-driven' must be resisted. The ideal public relations programme is proactive, not reactive.

The methodology of public relations is best expressed diagrammatically (Figure 1.1). Corporate objectives lead to shorter-term business plans, out of which, after careful assessment, a public relations strategy can be determined. While it has been stressed that ideally public relations will be proactive and programmed, it is true every day that reactive measures may become necessary to meet emergencies or harmful criticism.

The scheme shown in Figure 1.1 is developed further in Figure 1.2. Corporate objectives and business plans tend to be handed down at a fixed point in the corporate planning cycle. But the objectives can only be attained if they have been analysed in the light of political and social trends, changing issues, and the perceptions of the relevant sections of the public. It is through a study of public or group perceptions that it is possible to gauge

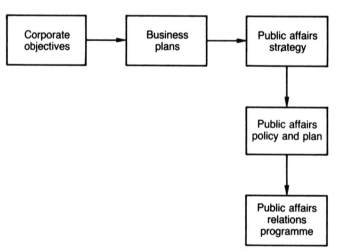

Figure 1.1 *Methodology of public relations*

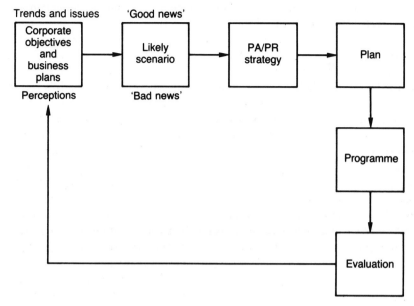

Figure 1.2 *Public relations methodology elaborated*

the amount of understanding and support a company is likely to receive for its plans and performance.

Issues management

This may appear to be a formidable title but Abraham Lincoln summed it up very neatly: 'If we could first know where we are and whither we are tending we could better judge what to do and how to do it'.

The term 'issues management' was first coined in 1977 by Howard Chase in the United States but the concept is not new. The following working definition explains its relevance: 'Issues management is identifying, analysing, developing positions, and briefing management on public policy issues that will have a critical effect on the company'. The critical point to note in this definition is its emphasis on the future. Issues management is concerned with forecasting the likely impact of issues and advising management on how to respond to them.

Perceptions

One must not lose sight of the basic factor, the public, without whom there would be no issues. It is through a study of perceptions held by relevant sections of the public that it is possible to gauge the support an organization is likely to receive for its policies and practices.

Trends and issues

Howard Chase has defined an issue as 'an unsettled matter which is ready for decision' and trends as 'detectable changes which precede issues'. Issues may be immediate, which most people would call crises, short-term or long-term. Issues can be perceptual, political, social, commercial or physical, even cultural, moral or ethical, or a mixture of all these. The list of possible issues is vast, but among issues that have recently become important to most organizations can be mentioned the environment and conservation, human rights and business ethics.

The study of forecasting issues and trends has become a science in itself but the extent to which it must be taken into account will depend on the type and scope of an organization.

It is useful to summarize the stages of issues management:

1 Create your own list of issues that appear to be on the move. Find them by being in touch, by asking around, by consulting.
2 Assign priorities to the list according to the time scale and the likelihood of the issue moving.
3 Validate your time scale with external sources you trust.
4 Set priorities according to the likely significance and impact on your organization.
5 Validate these priorities.
6 Discuss and validate your approach with key players internally – those in the organization who have a vested interest in the issue or whose support you need.
•7 Articulate on paper the opinions open to your organization for the management of the issue.
8 Try to get a consensus within the organization on the nature of the issue and the steps necessary to deal with it.
9 Now try to nominate the external target audience. If time permits, test the messages with representatives of the targets.
10 Finally, establish which corporate colleague is going to become responsible for the issue. Create and cost an action plan based on the likely time scale. Determine and publicize what the cost to the organization will be if nothing is done.

Before leaving this question of issues management, it is relevant to quote the Mexican Statement, which was signed by representatives of more than

thirty regional and national public relations associations gathered together
at Mexico City on 11 August 1978. The agreed definition reads as follows:

> Public relations practice is the art and social science of analysing trends,
> predicting their consequences, counselling organization's leadership, and
> implementing planned programmes of action which will serve both the
> organization's and the public interest.

Only when an institution's mission, objectives and business plans have
been reviewed and assessed in the light of perceptions (opinion research)
and trends and issues (issues management) is it possible to create the three
important scenarios – the 'good' news, the 'bad' news, and the 'line of best
fit'. Only then is it possible to calculate a strategy leading to a public
relations plan made up of project plans. Assuming objectives and benchmarks have been set, then 'evaluation' completes the management cycle and
the whole process starts again.

Using research

Professor Glen Broom, of San Diego State University, has indicated that the
use of research in public relations practice falls under five main headings:

1 Aimed specifically at planning or developing a new strategy, programme
   or activity.
2 Aimed at monitoring or tracking activities under way so as to assess
   desirable corrections or changes.
3 Evaluating outcomes, impact or effectiveness.
4 For publicity or promotional purposes.
5 In support of crisis management.

Dr Walter Lindemann, Director of Research of a New York consultancy,
has for many years been emphasizing the value of research in public
relations. He has recently suggested a novel way of distinguishing between
different levels of measurement of the results of public relations
programmes. He describes these different levels as 'outputs', 'outgrowths'
and 'outcomes'.

It is easy to measure 'outputs' by literature search and secondary analysis of data collected by others. There are now many systems available to
analyse and attempt to quantify the value of media relations.

'Outgrowths' describe the effects of a public relations programme after it
has been in operation for some time. To what extent are people taking notice
of the messages being disseminated and understanding and accepting the

arguments. These 'outgrowths' can be measured by a combination of qualitative and quantitative methods of data collection.

Lindemann emphasises that it is much more difficult to measure 'outcomes', which he describes as the extent to which people change their attitudes, opinions and habits.

A practical example of research

The context

The following 'story' is a typical example of a research challenge. 'You have just been appointed the public relations director to Universal Utilities plc, a London-based European 'multi-community' company with international ramifications, i.e. plants, marketing operations, joint ventures and strategic alliances. The company is a conglomerate in the sense that it provides financial services (banking, insurance and venture capital) and both consumer and industrial products.

The Consumer Products Division spans detergents, toiletries and kitchen equipment (white goods). The conglomerate's Industrial Division contains companies supplying the energy, chemical and aerospace industries with equipment and components. It has recently bought its way into the nuclear industry. The companies operate under their own names. Through its financial services, it has engaged in a substantial way, through joint ventures, in catering, security and office equipment. The work force of its core divisions number 110,000 and in joint ventures a further 50,000. The company has 20,000 pensioners.

Quoted on the stock exchanges in London, New York and Tokyo, it is estimated that the company's private shareholders number 120,000 and some 300 institutions hold 76 per cent of the shares. It manufactures in twenty-four countries and markets in ninety-three. It is further estimated that its suppliers number about 650 large and 3000 small to medium sized. The number of wholesalers and retailers it deals with worldwide is thought to be 10,000. The consumers of its Consumer Product Division number millions and the consumers of the Industrial Division run into thousands.

Its annual turnover is £2.5 billion and its trading profit was £1.3 million. Its dividends are in line with stock-market expectations. It pays out annually £5.5 billion to suppliers and it contributes about £2 billion in national, state, local and city taxes.

The Chairman, CEO, board and management are well respected, and succession is assured. The board has expressed itself recently as 'not happy with our public image' and rightly or wrongly the recently retired public relations manager is blamed.

The Chairman, while happy with the share price and the attitude of the financial commentators, nevertheless believes that the investing community does not appreciate the significance of the company's record of performance and the security derived from its commercial activities. The CEO sees ahead a degree of restructuring, some divestment, some plant closures, and some redundancies, balanced by diversifications and acquisitions. Both officers feel strongly that if their corporate strategy is to be realized successfully, a wider and deeper understanding of the company's plans is essential.

You have been instructed to leave the routine operation of the public relations department in the hands of your competent deputy for the present and to devote all your time and effort to making a study of the situation and to prepare to make a presentation to the main board in three months' time. This should be a succinct review of the situation with recommendations for action. Within reason, all the resources you require to complete this task professionally will be available to you.

How are you going to approach this task? What are you going to do? The CEO would like to approve your plan before you begin and would like you to explain what is to be done.

Before you can start to create a corporate public relations strategy, plan and programme, what desk, formal, qualitative and quantitative research will you want the answers to?

To prepare for your meeting with the CEO, make out a list of the kind of activities you wish to undertake during these three months.

The checklist

The challenge can be approached under eight headings:

1 *Corporate level*
- Study the corporate mission statement:
  Objectives.
  Strategic plan.
  Business plans.
  Component plans.
- Preliminary listing of political/social/economic/issues papers. Study of corporate discussion/policy/position papers.
- Reading/analysis of any existing research results.
- Historical, literary, library check on references.
- Record of legal actions as plaintiffs or defendants.
- Review of financial reports – bankers, brokers, analysts, institutions, commentators.

- Review and analysis of past media coverage of industry sectors within which the company works.
- Negotiation and consultation record.
- Fair business policies and practices. Business ethics.
- Quality and excellence programmes.

2 *Operational level*

- Internal communication standards and methods.
- Enquiry and complaint procedures/handling/reports.
- Visitor- and guest-handling levels.
- Telephone/correspondence/interview-handling/records.

3 *Communications level*

- IDENTITY: plant, vehicles, print, personnel, products, etc.
- MATERIAL: statements, releases, announcements:
  Print and publicity.
  Audio-visual material.
  Information and educational material.
  Advertising
- ACTIVITIES:
  Executive – public contact points/levels.
  Executive – community involvement.
  Employee – community involvement
  Community service programme.
  Social sponsorship and responsibility policies/programme
- POLICIES
  Review of rationale and content of existing communication policies, programmes, themes, targets.
  Budgets.
  Outside advisers and suppliers.

4 *Intelligence phase*

- Refinement of issues, including definition of time-frame, establishment of the necessary decision process, nominations of main role players, articulation of own and opponents' case, listing of key contacts and target individuals and groups.
- Qualitative and quantitative research among stakeholders, key.contacts, relevant opinion leaders and general public, to establish awareness levels and perceptions held bearing on image/reputation credibility.
- Establish inter-firm comparisons in regard to image/reputation and credibility/awareness.
- Study of opinion and attitudinal research concerning industry sectors within which the company operates.
- Review of political, social, economic, cultural and moral environment in the company's main production and market countries.

- Check on level and degree of contact between company representatives and nominate key contacts and targets.
- Scenario creation exercise begins.

5 *Creative phase*

- Internal focus groups with executives and selected employees to establish gap between (1) what they *believe* the public is, and (2) what (in honesty) they *think* the company deserves it to be. External and stakeholder focus groups to supplement quantitative research into image, reputation, credibility.
- GAP LEVELS between

Desired image	and	actual image.
Issue policy	and	corporate performance.
Communications claims	and	corporate delivery.
External perceptions	and	actual performance.
External norms	and	corporate performance.

- Assessment of degree of corporate public:
    communications (two-way).
    dialogue.
    Preliminary listing of corporate policies and practices in need of modification.
    Articulation of public relations targets and themes.

6 *Programming phase*

- Pretesting and pilot target testing of communications themes and messages.
- Pilot testing of proposed activities and audience response and reactions.

7 *Personal schedule*

- Structured series of one-on-one meetings/interviews with (*internally*) selected corporate executives at staff, line and field levels, and (*externally*) with representatives of stakeholders and 'supporters' and 'opponents' of company policies, performance and plans, plus representatives of obvious 'intermediaries' and acknowledged 'third party endorsers'.

8 *Ongoing activity*

- Continued testing of messages and activities.
- Agreement of communications objectives.
- Agreement of responses/reactions sought.
- Agreement of 'benchmarks'.
- Establishment of 'indicators'.
- Evaluation.

The reaction of the CEO?

The CEO may be surprised by the wide scope of the proposed public relations investigation. However, if he was asking for a study of all aspects of corporate governance, this is the type of detailed analysis he would expect to receive. Apart from giving an example of the complex study required to answer the company's brief, this scenario emphasizes that there is much more to public relations practice than merely media relations.

Summary

This chapter has described the rationale and methodology of public relations practice. The way it operates in specific circumstances will be described in detail in other chapters.

Professor James Grunig, of the University of Maryland, has identified four different models of practice. The early press agency and publicity was succeeded by the public information phase, which concentrated on giving information and orders in a one-way method of communication. Practitioners following these two models regard their purpose as talking rather than listening.

The third model is described by Grunig as two-way asymmetric. This accepts the importance of dialogue and the establishment of mutual understanding but expects the public to modify its attitudes and opinions. Only in the fourth two-way symmetric model is there a balance between the interests of the organization and those of its publics, and a willingness to modify policies if necessary.

The four-model concept is useful in describing the different spheres of a typical public relations programme but often one or more of these types of practice will be used simultaneously by an organization in its internal and external relations.

In order to promulgate its messages and gathering audience responses, a company may employ a communications mix comprising any or all of the following techniques: media relations, advertising, publicity and print, direct mailing, exhibitions, special events, visits, speeches and statements, published position papers, reports and specialized research, briefings, seminars and conferences, interviews, professional affairs programmes, community programmes, employee communications and an active networking system. All this constitutes 'public relations in action'.

2

Media relations

Phyllis Oberman

Successful public relations depends on effective communication with a wide variety of audiences, or publics. The most important method of communication is through media relations and liaison.

Like public relations in general, media relations is both proactive and reactive. If a company or organization is large enough or newsworthy, the media will be interested and will monitor its progress and actions. The choice is between seeking to work with the journalists or keeping them at arm's length. The advantage of cooperating with the media is that the stories they publish are more likely to be accurate and sympathetic.

In this chapter, I am dealing mostly with proactive media relations, as reactive situations dictate their own agenda. Effective media relations is essentially one of the main means by which organizations communicate their objectives. Types of media range from all forms of the printed word to international communications via computerized satellite systems such as the Internet.

Media relations must always be viewed as an integral part of a total public relations programme and never something bolted on at the end. It is also never the object itself. Effectiveness is only achieved if it is conveying the right message via the right media to the right audience.

Sources of information

There is no substitute for thorough research before getting down to planning a media relations campaign. Learning the research techniques needed will save endless hours and, more importantly, help avoid poorly targeted material.

In most developed countries there are media reference directories and publications, and information available on computerized disc. Data are ready to hand on readership profiles outlining the types and life-styles of the readers or viewers, advance planning schedules of publications and TV production companies, viewing and listening figures, circulating figures, and much else. Public relations professionals really have little excuse for wrongly or inaccurately targeted information.

As all forms of media develop and divide into more and more segments, offering specialized subject matter for particular audiences, in a sense it becomes easier for public relations practitioners to reach their key target audiences. A glance at the category headings in any of the leading media directories will substantiate this point. In the consumer field categories of print media might range from angling and fishing to wine, beer and spirits. In the trade and technical area you could find subjects ranging from accountancy to water and sewage, with such things as meat trade, metal industries, mining and quarrying, in between.

Media matrix

TV, radio, and the commercially printed media make up the bulk of media generally most relevant in public relations. However, internal publications or house journals reach vast numbers of people. Existing publications may be important to a particular programme. In another project it might be preferable to research the potential for the setting up of a new, one-off or regular publication. The creation of a new medium to carry a particular message could well form part of a planned public relations programme.

A growth sector in many countries with sophisticated distribution and retailing systems is that of sponsored customer magazines – some highly glossy and paid for in up-market supermarkets, others given away at trade counters, e.g. to builders or electricians, or mailed as part of the subscription to a professional or special-interest organization. These specialized forms of media all have a role to play and are worth seeking out where they are demonstrably relevant.

Relevance and influence

Proper media reseach will aid the structuring and maintenance of a relevant media relations campaign.

While professional public relations people have done much to dispel the myth of the importance of column inches as such, there is still a long way to go in persuading many clients or managements that what is important is how the media have influenced the audiences that have been targeted. How effective has the media relations programme been in changing attitudes of key audiences, or in influencing sales or pressure groups in their view of a given situation?

As the realization that the impact of a public relations campaign is much more important than the mere output in terms of column inches or sheer coverage, then the relevance of media evaluation systems grows. Pre- and post-research on public relations campaigns has historically been confined mostly to big-budget programmes managed by executives convinced about and familiar with the use of research.

Now there are specialist companies offering a wide variety of evaluation services in various price ranges and these are expanding. Some public relations consultancies run their own in-house systems.

One organization now offers public relations practitioners a service that has been used by certain more sophisticated advertisers for some years, by means of the techniques of a discipline called semiotics, which researches and evaluates the 'hidden meanings' of companies' activities and messages, looking into and setting out what they call the 'body language' of a campaign. It remains to be seen whether semiotic analysis will gain credence among public relations practitioners.

Being crystal clear about the objectives of a public relations programme and equally clear about the key publics at whom the campaign is aimed, and with whom a dialogue is desirable, is an essential requirement for developing effective media relations. Once clearly agreed, then the forms of media to be used can be much more accurately pinpointed.

For example, an article in the *Financial Times* reported on some new research into UK population ages and suggested that a 22 per cent fall will have taken place by the year 2001 in people aged between fifteen and twenty-nine, while a 22 per cent rise in the numbers aged between fifty and fifty-nine will be achieved by that year. The implications of this to high street retail stores or house builders, for example, is very interesting and is no doubt being studied carefully by them. Many firms are initiating their own research programmes to probe more deeply into this development.

Successful media owners, particularly in print media, have grasped the potential of profitable magazine sales aimed at the 'grey' market. House builders saw the prospects for mid- and up-market housing aimed at this sector, though it is still a modest development in the UK compared to that of the United States. Radio and television have maintained generally a broad-brush appeal, with little, as yet, aimed at this specific audience.

Public relations practitioners working on behalf of companies and organizations whose marketing efforts are aimed at the 'greys' will find that research into target media will pay dividends in influencing this sector, whose spending power is often overlooked, except by companies marketing specialized financial services.

Research, read, listen, view

Researching and accurately targeting the correct media are the key first steps in media relations. Next come reading the publications, and listening or looking at radio or TV programmes. Familiarity with the editorial requirements for information, illustrated by way of pictures, photo-opportunities, sound 'bites' and video clips, is crucial. Editors and programme producers, often quite justifiably, complain that public relations people do not bother to find out what their particular needs are. This sort of essential attention to detail is time-consuming but pays long-term dividends.

Freelances and specialist writers and programme-makers

A slimmed down media structure has led to smaller staffs or no staff on many publications, with the editor buying in commissioned feature and news material from outside freelances. In television similar slimming down has meant that while programme-making staff have been reduced considerably, the number of independent programme-making companies has proliferated.

In some sectors the key freelance writers are fairly well documented in the media directories. In other sectors research and detective work become necessary to identify these people and make contact with them. The maintenance of regular contact with key freelance journalists is an area which, perhaps because of the hard labour required, is often given scant attention.

Independent TV-programme-making companies are listed to some extent in specialist directories, and there are regular publications detailing coming programmes or series, some of which may have relevance to public relations practitioners.

Video news releases

VNRs are video versions of press releases designed to offer television broadcasters background pictures to help cover a story. This is the simple explanation by VNR firm Medialink for this new development in media relations. It is an extension of the service that has been available for many years for the distribution of taped material on cassette to radio stations.

Video news releases are issued by an increasing number of specialist companies on behalf of government departments, major corporations and non-profit organizations such as charities.

As TV outlets grow on a worldwide basis the opportunities to contribute news and feature material via VNRs expands accordingly, permitting the public relations operator to reach ever wider audiences. The video news releases companies also offer the possibility of international satellite link-ups for key spokespeople to be interviewed live on TV around the world.

BBC World Service Television provides a worldwide satellite TV service in Europe, Asia, Africa and Japan, with 300 correspondents worldwide. This expansion also offers the public relations practitioner media opportunities worth investigating.

Wire services

Public relations wire services have also grown in importance, and in Britain specialist firms offer every aspect of the production and distribution of news and feature material emanating from public relations sources – both in the UK and overseas. Multinational teams of journalists customize public relations material to suit media in overseas countries and arrange translation where necessary. Links have been formed between the public relations wire services and traditional news agencies.

An interesting new development in the area of electronic media is an organization called the WORLD PRESS CENTRE (WPC) based in London. This is an electronic, online service that distributes information from government and international agencies, campaigning groups, public relations organizations and commercial companies. It is not a news agency. The system puts the material on editors' and TV producers' screens in the form in which it is received by WORLD PRESS CENTRE.

The WPC computer system organizes the information it receives into dozens of different categories – not just by subject matter but also by geographic area and by type of material. This ranges from items such as press conference announcements to background briefings on companies or specialist topics.

A specialist journalist can therefore set up his system to identify all material available on, say, climatic change anywhere in the world. Another special correspondent might demand company financial results in Japan.

Organizations such as the World Bank, Oxfam, the European Commission and Unesco are already using this system, and WORLD PRESS CENTRE claims that its newsroom retrieval system will be in use by media throughout the world within a few years. Subscriptions and the specially designed software are costed very reasonably.

While WPC appears to be the only organization offering this service at the time of writing, it seems likely that similar schemes will be developed as access to information worldwide by means of specialist computer software continues to grow.

Words and Pictures

'A picture is worth a thousand words' is a well-known saying. The importance of photography to illustrate public relations material aimed at the print media is often underrated.

Picture editors of print media and news agencies have very particular needs and standards. Careful study of the illustration policy of target publications should always precede the commissioning of photography to accompany a news or feature release.

Editors can often be approached and consulted in advance of an expensive photographic session. With some publications it is sometimes possible to negotiate and sponsor editorial photography without damaging the publication's editorial integrity.

The question of payment by public relations practitioners as a condition for the publication of colour photographs, and the extension of this practice to other material submitted for editorial consideration, has become a vexed one. All the parties concerned, represented by their professional associations, continue to debate the long-term implications of this blurring of the demarcation between editorial columns and paid advertising, which is considered a serious threat to journalistic integrity as well as that of public relations practitioners, publishing and advertising.

Media relations – key tasks

- To source information on media and maintain up-to-date files/subscribe
- to media information services.
- To coordinate advance editorial schedules of relevant print media, radio and TV.
- To maintain continually updated information on key contacts in the media through personal liaison.
- To maintain personal contacts with editors and programme producers relevant to your own work.
- To research and build up files on specialist freelance contacts in relevant fields.
- To keep abreast of new channels of communication and to evaluate their relevance for public relations practitioners.
- To be aware of all useful reference material on the media and ensure you are always up to date with new media and developments.

Conclusion

Communication is an ever moving and changing scene. New media are continuously being invented and reinvented, and the public relations practitioner who wishes to conduct media relations efficiently must strive to keep ahead of this movement.

3

Other media of public relations – exhibitions, words and images

Betty Dean

Among the other media of public relations are exhibitions, and these are backed by words and images. Public relations programmes in all their forms enhance and support the corporate plan of the organization. They should have both short-term and long-term aims and are an essential element of the marketing, finance, personnel and production goals of a commerical company. In the non-commercial sector public relations techniques play an integral part in the dissemination of ideas and information to the organiza-tion's target audiences.

Exhibitions can be of many different types, ranging from trade and consumer shows to trade fairs and private events. They can be used to promote all areas of company activity, provided that the event is properly researched and identified as being appropriate for the task in hand. The Exhibition Liaison Committee has produced a very useful brochure, which looks at the industry background and opportunities available to the poten-tial exhibitor. It is available from ISBA (Incorporated Society of British Advertisers), 44 Hertford Street, London W1Y 8AE.

All exhibitions incorporate the written and spoken word in the form of brochures, news releases, seminar papers and face-to-face interaction. Equally, the stand and brochure design and graphics carry important visual messages about the company and the way it sees itself in relation to its publics. This chapter looks at words and images in a general way in their application to all public relations activities.

Public relations programmes aim to modify existing attitudes or to intro-duce new ideas that will be of value to the organization sponsoring the public relations activities. This will usually call for the use of several media to reach the target publics. Different media may be employed at different times or all the media may be used together in concert. The media of public relations include relationships with the press, radio and television, which are usually described as 'media relations', and which is described in Chapter 2.

The marketing programme of many organizations will include participation in exhibitions or trade fairs. The objective may be to publicize and sell products and services or to provide a meeting place with existing or potential customers.

Once a decision has been made to participate in a particular event, it can become the responsibility of the public relations department to carry out the detailed planning and to see the whole operation through to a successful conclusion. This responsibility does, however, depend on the particular structure of a company. It can be a marketing responsibility.

The exhibition business

Exhibition companies operate in the service sector. Their mission statements incorporate the concepts of being 'facilitators of free trade' and 'generators of business for commerce and industry'.

They can be likened to publishing houses – where many of the major exhibition companies' roots lie – in that they own a series of titles. Just as magazines, they are carefully researched, named and packaged to meet perceived gaps in niche markets.

As with all brands, a number of similar sounding titles tend to emerge under competitors' banners once an exhibition has established itself in the market place. This is good news for exhibitors, since it leads to the provision of better services and facilities at conference centres.

In such a competitive environment exhibition organizers seek ways of providing better media opportunities and exhibitor support. Equally, the decision-making process is assisted by the market research data, which is readily available to exhibitors in the form of detailed attendance figures and visitor profiles. However, one of the disadvantages of competitive events is the fragmentation of industry focus.

The exhibition industry is a complex business. Its primary purpose is to promote an idea and to sell floor space. It provides a wide variety of ancillary services – stand designers and contractors, engineering services, photographers, caterers, florists, furniture suppliers, printers, cleaning staff and security personnel – and is underpinned by substantial marketing, advertising and public relations activity.

Exhibition development

The exhibition industry is also an evolving business. In the 1950s and 1960s 'glamour' exhibitions such as the Motor Show were events in the social calendar – an opportunity to meet friends. A complimentary ticket to visit an exhibitor's stand was as much a prized status symbol as a designer label is today.

In the 1990s business is hard-nosed and the market place is a global village with all its different cultural conventions. Exhibitions have to be more than opportunities to facilitate social contact. The exhibition concept has developed from being a showcase for goods and services to a multi-faceted media 'theme scheme', which may have its origins in a television programme, as happened with Clothes Show Live.

In 1989 the producers of the TV programme 'The Clothes Show' came up with the idea of creating a live event and exhibition around the programme. A specialist independent event-organizing company, Barker Brown Ltd, was approached and took on the task. The advantages of this event were the following: the potential target publics had been identified through the programme's audience research profile, the name was well-known, and the high profile presenters, Jeff Banks and Selina Scott, were prepared to be associated with the project.

For first time exhibitors at 'Clothes Show Live', the partnership between the different media forms minimized the risks inherent in participating in a new exhibition. Exhibitors were assured of high media interest and coverage – both electronic and printed – and it was possible to estimate attendance figures and visitor profile breakdown with a high degree of accuracy.

Exhibition organization

As the exhibition industry has become more global, the approach to setting up and marketing these events has changed. For instance, Mack Brooks Exhibitions used to service all their overseas shows from the UK, including press office staff. Now mainland European and overseas exhibitions rely on the services of local public relations and marketing consultants. Press offices are staffed by indigenous personnel who have a clear understanding of the requirements of the national and regional media. They are thus able to provide a first class service to exhibitors.

Exhibition objectives

There are various types of exhibition, ranging from road shows to private, consumer and trade, and technical events. It is a public relations responsibility to identify the appropriate event in order to achieve maximum benefit from exhibition participation. Lists of forthcoming home and overseas exhibitions are given in *Overseas Trade*, published quarterly by the Department of Trade and Industry, and in trade publications such as

Exhibition Bulletin. There is no satisfactory substitute, however, for personal knowledge of an event.

Successful exhibiting must start with a clear definition of the desired results from participation. The next step is to identify the most likely event that will enable the company to achieve these objectives and to agree this with the client or employer.

When a decision has been reached to participate in a particular event, a detailed programme has to be agreed. This starts with deciding how large a stand is required to show off all the exhibits to advantage, and selecting the best available site in the exhibition hall.

A critical path analysis will ensure that the stand will be ready on time, complemented by the advertising and marketing activities that will ensure the success of the operation. A comprehensive public relations programme should always be mounted in support of participation in any exhibition, large or small. Attention should be given to the appearance of the stand, the attitude of the stand staff and the way in which enquiries are handled, as all these contribute towards the reputation and corporate image of the exhibiting company.

DTI financial assistance

A company exhibiting overseas for the first time can participate in a Department of Trade and Industry Trade Fairs Support Scheme. This offers considerable financial assistance for the first three participations in an approved overseas trade fair. This is extended to five events in selected markets. Companies participate under the British flag and the section is organized by a trade association, a chamber of commerce or other approved non-profit-making body. Many British companies have been introduced to the international market place by this very successful DTI initiative.

A case study

A British company that benefited from participation in the British section of an overseas trade fair was IAC Limited. The company had won a NATO contract for producing engine test houses for the Tornado KB199. Following this foray into the overseas market under the auspices of the DTI, the company won contracts from armed services worldwide.

However, this success was not easily won. A considerable public relations effort went into ensuring the success of this first incursion into the world of overseas exhibiting. Using the shell structure provided by the DTI, the stand was designed to attract the eye and to enhance the IAC corporate image. An attractive brochure was designed to complement the stand graphics and a special tie carried an adaptation of the main graphic motif. These ties eventually gained cult status in the industry.

As usual at exhibitions these days, a seminar was held during the exhibition and the company's Aviation Director, George Dawson, was accepted as a speaker. The firm's public relations officer wrote the draft outline of the speech, which was later published in the ,*Seminar Proceedings* and distributed worldwide.

Additionally, news releases had been written, cleared and expertly translated into German and French by native speakers of these languages. Feature articles were written and sent to the Exhibition's Press Officer for use in the *Exhibition Newsletter* and for placement with journalists. A media list of specific magazines and journalists for follow up was drawn up and press packs were prepared both for the exhibition press office and for appropriate visitors to the stand.

Invitations were sent to existing and potential customers and all enquiries received at the exhibition were carefully recorded for 'thank you' letters to be sent and follow up after the team's return to the UK. In order to maximize media interest, news releases were sent out to the national, and trade and technical, press before, during and after the event. Media coverage was monitored and evaluated to previously agreed criteria.

Some of the sales leads were applicable to other divisions of the company and these were passed on to the Sales Director for further action. All that remained was to total all the invoices and to make sure that the end result was within budget. The final stage was the preparation of a detailed evaluation report.

Participation in any exhibition, home or overseas, is very expensive, particularly when full allowance is made for administration and staff time. Even with DTI financial assistance, the total cost is likely to be very high. This emphasizes the importance of good planning and the effective public relations support that can make such a difference to the success of participation in any event.

So the golden rule is to research the event thoroughly and to ensure that it meets corporate, marketing and sales objectives. Do not forget the small but vital points such as ordering furniture, cleaning and taking out insurance. Return all the exhibitor's forms within the time scale and provide a suitable entry for the exhibition catalogue.

Words

As the song says, 'Words don't come easy...' Well, that's true when we are seeking to convey deeply held beliefs and feelings in either spoken or written language. It is also true when we try to simplify complex concepts into every-day English. When we use words, we are expressing our perception of the world in which we live. We use words as a shorthand for ideas and experience. When we speak and when we write in run of the mill social interaction, we are telling the person receiving the communication who we are and what we stand for. We bring our attitudes, prejudices and predispositions into the public arena by our choice of words.

In business situations we often dehumanize ourselves and the information by using jargon. The spoken word is transient; there is an immediacy of response. The desired effect or reaction is dependent on the speaker's ability to find the right words at the right time in order to create a relationship with the listener. The words are supported by tone of voice, body language and the surrounding environment. At its most eloquent, spoken language triggers a resonance within the listener on the shared experienced of the human condition.

But the written word has no physical intermediary present to clarify what is on paper. It relies on the skill of the writer to transmit thoughts and ideas through the medium of symbols on a page. There are no second chances; once the words appear in written form and are read by another person the writer is committed.

The most technically difficult writing form is poetry. With a few carefully chosen words and working within a disciplined structure, the poet endeavours to distil intense personal experience to convey abstract ideas and complex thought.

Words are the tools of the trade, assisted by linguistic devices such as phonology, morphology, syntax and semantics. The sounds of language, word inflection and formation, sentence construction, the meanings of words and their ability to evolve become the vehicle for denoting change in social attitudes and perceptions.

But sometimes the language we use is not appropriate for the job. Research into the 'readability' of chemistry textbooks undertaken by B C Slater and J J Thompson in the 1980s found that the average reading age of the books was far above the average age of the student. Sentence length ranged from 7 to 70 words in some science textbooks. 'In most cases, science is not the problem, it is the language of science that is the difficulty. Many students find science lessons almost as incomprehensible as French or Greek'.[1]

Jargon, or the language of the professions, is designed to be elitist and ensure that outsiders stay outside the magic circle. It is also thought to convey complicated concepts in totality, without change in meaning, across generations and countries. But as word association tests have shown[2], cultural references create yet another barrier. Scottish students when looking at the scientific term 'states of matter' (gas, liquid or solid) thought of countries and states, while Malaysian students focused on the literal translation of 'state' into the local word *rupabentuk*, which means 'shape' or 'face'.

We of course are not academics, we are professional communicators – public relations practitioners. We can plead 'not guilty' to charges of creating and disseminating material that is not clear and concise. If we do not use the written word in a form appropriate to our target publics, we cannot consider ourselves to be professionals in the field of communication.

Chrissie Maher is founder of the 'Plain English Campaign', whose stated aim is 'to stamp out all forms of gobbledygook, legalese, small print and bureaucratic language'. As she says, 'Communication has only one purpose – to get information from one person to another successfully'. To this end the organization has set up a quality control scheme under the Crystal Mark label.

The Crystal Mark shows that the document has reached a high standard of clarity in its language and layout. Among the things it looks for are:

- A good average sentence length (about 15 to 20 words).
- Plenty of 'active' verbs.
- Everyday English.
- Conciseness.
- Clear, helpful headings, with consistent and suitable ways of making them stand out from the text.
- Good type size and clear typeface.
- An average line length of between 7 and 12 words.

These are all the ingredients of a good tabloid newspaper. The *Daily Mirror*, which informs its readers of the world about them in very direct and everyday English, has its own 'What' triangle:

W
Who
What
Why
Where
When
H
How did it happen?
What are the implications?
A
Additional information

T
Tie up loose ends.

The first sentence covers WHAT happened in not more than 14 – 18 words.

It is extremely demanding to write in the simplistic tabloid newspaper style. It requires a knowledge and love of language to put across complex ideas in an easily accessible way, without losing the essence of the message.

This is what we need to practise in our dealings with our various publics. We are not there to cloud issues and to demonstrate how clever we are, but to convey information and arguments in the most straightforward manner. Language, both spoken and written, is a control mechanism. Euphemism and metaphor can be used to disguise harsh truths, e.g. 'ethnic cleansing' or 'genetic engineering', distancing reality and allaying fear. It can be used to generate a climate of acceptance and to change the face of our world. It can also be a power enhancer, viz. the feminist gender argument.

House journals and newsletters

These style and language considerations also apply to house journals and newsletters, one of the most frequent uses of the printed word in public relations programmes.

A reference database

A valuable reference source of contemporary spoken and written British English words and text is currently being put on to a database 'Communicators in Business'. It is likely to be the largest computerized language research tool in the world. It is part of a collaborative venture between the British National Corpus of Current English, Larousse, the Longman Group and the Univerities of Oxford and Lancaster. The information will provide future generations with a snapshot of life in Great Britain towards the end of the millennium.

Some 100 million words, taken from personal letters, speech, commercial documents and technical reports, will be classified and coded. This material will be made available for academic study and communication reference books. One of the other objectives is to ensure that English technical and commercial terminology, which is being used increasingly throughout the world, retains its root meaning. However, in order to do this the terms first have to be explained in plain English, and as we said before, words don't come easy.

Images

Images are powerful, whether carved, cast, drawn, photographic or computer-generated. In less literate and media-oriented times the symbol was one of the few opportunities for uncensored trans-cultural communication. It crossed land and sea, bringing with it new ideas.

Symbols are visual metaphors. The fish represents the bonding wish of the early Christian church, a political ideology is personified by a hammer and sickle device, resistance to oppression is expressed through the lighted candle encircled by a ring of barbed wire used by Amnesty International.

The chosen visual representation not only encompasses shared values, but also empowers the individual. Association with the symbol brings strength through numbers; it is an affirmation of kinship. One does not stand alone.

In Elizabethan times, symbolism was all-important. A skull in a painting did not just represent death. The juxtaposition of other objects on the canvas carried clear messages to the viewer and keyed into the mass consciousness and perception of the age. Today, we convey these messages through the use of high technology, particularly in the superimposition of images using computer graphics and combining multi-media techniques, as for example in pop videos.

Given this hidden agenda, when we have the responsibility of assisting in the choice or updating of a corporate identity logo or brand label, we need to enlist all the help available. As communication professionals, we should be open to expert advice from industrial psychologists, market researchers, designers and typographers.

We are lucky enough to have research available, research that has investigated colour psychology, perception and cultural association, and it is up to us to use this information. It is no easy task to design a symbol that can represent the corporate ethos and, at the same time, engender shared values among a disparate audience. If the corporate image requires explanation, it is not doing its job.

Imagery is all around us, and, in general, people are far more visually aware than they were before television and video recorders became part of the furniture. Computer-literate youngsters pick up visual signals and connotations very quickly, while the older public is still busy trying to work out the significance of the juxtaposed elements, be they electronic or printed.

Public relations practitioners must have sufficient knowledge and experience of the electronic and printed media in order to achieve the best results for their employers or clients. This requires at least an awareness of the terminology used within the disciplines of video, TV, radio, design, print and photography and an understanding of the advantages and constraints of the chosen medium.

You cannot brief a photographer unless you have learnt to appreciate a well-composed picture. Knowledge of where and how the picture is being used; the required format, portrait, landscape or square; what lighting is required and whether power sources are available for outdoor work; colour or black and white film and how many shots are required; form the basic background information that the photographer needs to have in order to produce a good result. Once you have briefed the photographer, be on location to ensure that all the necessary facilities are available, but remember that you have selected the photographer to do the job for you and do not interfere once shooting has started.

With the increasing sophistication of design and the numerous software packages available for computer graphics, a montage approach to visual imagery has become increasingly popular. It all becomes perhaps stylized and somewhat anodyne. What of the future? All this symbolism, on its long journey from cave drawings and pictures on a church wall, to television and computer screens, but where will it end? Marcia Kuperberg, Director of West Herts College School of Media is looking at the 'shiny new world of multimedia' the time will come when instead of reading a newspaper, magazine or book, we will take up a CD-ROM disk. This will be played on a computer with an in-built or connected CD-ROM drive, sound card and speakers. We can then bring text to life, using light, sound and image.

Marcia gives an example from *Grolier's Academic American Encyclopaedia*, when, to see how birds fly, the appropriate CD-ROM (which contains 650 mb, the equivalent of some 800 floppy disks) is inserted into the computer. This shows the process in words and moving pictures, with a slow-motion stop-frame video segment appearing on the computer screen. A sound card will then give access to birdsong.

The next stage is 'virtual reality', with a sensor glove enabling the viewer to walk among the trees and to interact with nature without leaving the house – total involvement without responsibility.

This new technology has heavy ethical implications for future public relations professionals.

References

1   Hogg, I. (1985) Postgraduate Research 1984 – 1985, PGCE, Leeds University.
2   Slater, B.C. and Thompson, J.S. (1984) *Educational Chemistry, Volume 3.*

4

Public affairs and corporate relations

Rosemary Graham

Introduction and definitions

What is public affairs? What is public relations? What is lobbying? How, if at all, does public affairs differ from public relations? To answer these questions we need to look at definitions of terms. Definitions abound in public relations. Some are helpful, others less so. This chapter also discusses definitions of public affairs and, given that practitioners define public relations every day by what they do,[1] the activities of public affairs managers are also defined. The current political climate within the UK – the backdrop against which public affairs practitioners perform their duties – is set out, and the major themes and factors shaping the political agenda are summarized. Ethical guidelines for public relations practice are also set out.

Definitions of public relations

There seems in some quarters today to be a reluctance to use the words 'public relations' because the term is considered somewhat discredited. Other terms are used increasingly to describe the public relations function – 'public affairs', 'marketing communication', 'corporate communication', 'issues management', 'external relations' and other variations. The Public Relations Society of America (PRSA) in a 1988 report concluded that there was no really satisfactory alternative term to 'public relations'.[2] The report proposes that public relations is an umbrella term that encompasses numerous specialist areas such as corporate communications and public affairs.

The PRSA offers several definitions of public relations, one of which in my view is particularly useful: 'Public relations helps organizations effectively interact and communicate with their key publics'. In short, public relations is concerned with the management of relationships.

Definition of public affairs

Defining public relations makes it easier to attempt a definition of public affairs. Public affairs is a comparatively new function in many UK companies. 'Little has been published on either theory or practice to build the base for a professional approach. As research reveals, there is considerable difference between leading practitioners about what the function involves.'[3] Some practitioners take a narrow view of public affairs, seeing it as equivalent to government relations and lobbying only. Other practitioners take a much broader view of the function and list eight separate activities as coming within the aegis of public affairs:

1 Issues management.
2 Government relations.
3 Community relations (including social responsibility and fund-giving).
4 Investor relations.
5 Media relations.
6 Publications.
7 Employee communication.
8 Corporate advertising (advocacy advertising).[4]

The definition of public affairs which perhaps sits most easily with the above PRSA definition is 'Public affairs is a specialist area of practice within public relations. It is concerned with those relationships which are involved in the development of public policy, legislation and regulation which may affect organisations, their interests and operations'.[5] One, but only one of these 'concerns' of public affairs as set out in this definition is legislation and this brings us to a definition of 'lobbying'.

Definition of lobbying

Kotler defines lobbying thus: 'Lobbying involves dealing with legislators and government officials to promote or defeat legislation or regulation'.[6] Clearly therefore lobbying is a specialized subset of public affairs but it is *not* the whole story in terms of the public affairs function, and cannot and should not be used as a synonym for public affairs.

Lobbying practices

Just as the term 'public relations' is seen in some quarters to be devalued, lobbying also has pejorative connotations. There is therefore an increasing tendency for 'lobbyists' to shy away from that title and to turn to the designation 'political consultant'.

In the USA

There is an increasing contrast between the connotations attributed to the word lobbyist in the UK and the USA. In the USA lobbying, if not considered an altogether noble profession, is at least viewed as a legitimate and respectable activity and is a huge industry. In fact recent numerous impasses in the US Congress, and failures on the part of the administration to secure approval for legislative proposals, have been partly attributed to the number and enormous influence of the diverse lobby groups in the USA. The gun lobby and private health care interests, to name but two, are groups that in their respective ways have managed to thwart presidential endeavours over many years to regulate ownership of firearms and health services.

In the UK

The UK has experienced a very sharp growth in the number of pressure groups actively campaigning here. Many have 'green' or environmental objectives in mind. While some of these organizations are considered to be cranky, not to say extreme, very many are viewed with sneaking admiration. Those environmentalists who recently camped on the roof of the home of John MacGregor, former Secretary of State for Transport, to protest about road-building plans and in the process gained prime time TV coverage were secretly admired by many political observers as enterprising publicity-seekers who successfully hit their target.

While the amateur enthusiasts, of which these pressure groups are composed, are often held in grudging regard on the part of civil servants and politicians. Sir Peter Kemp, former Permanent Secretary in the Cabinet Office and in charge of Whitehall's 'Next Steps' programme has said there is 'a vague impression of something being wrong with the activity of lobbying, of there being a slight smell of corruption about it, and that, seen from Whitehall, lobbyists are 'rather suspect animals'. While he stressed that this rather puritanical approach on the part of civil servants was increasingly dated, there is nevertheless a problem here to be addressed by those engaged in the lobbying function.[7]

Potential abuses

The right to make representation to Parliament is one of the basic prerogatives of a democracy – as precious as the right to vote. It is an honourable activity and a very important and necessary one. It has to be asked therefore what has gone wrong with this process to bring it into the disrepute it now seems to enjoy in the UK? A major cause for concern would seem to be the activities of a small minority of parliamentary consultancies and public relations agencies that offer advice on parliamentary affairs and, in the process, employ parliamentarians as advisers.

Some of these organisations have, on occasion, been accused of infringing what is regarded as proper parliamentary practice as set out in Erskine May's *Parliamentary Practice* (8th edition). Members of the Institute of Public Relations and the Public Relations Consultants Association who retain parliamentarians must, according to their professional codes of conduct, declare the fact and register the object of their retainer in books that are filed each year in the library of the House.

Members of Parliament asking a question or speaking to a motion on the floor of the House must first declare their interest, and particularly a financial interest, in a topic. Having done that, the parliamentarian is then free to say what he likes, although his objectivity may be compromised in the eyes of his peer group. Safeguards are in place to protect against abuse of the system but abuses there have been. An example of potential abuse in 1994 was the high profile case of two junior members of the government who alleged entrapment by the media to accept money for asking parliamentary questions. The furore to which this incident gave rise resulted in the immediate suspension from the government of both MPs.

The consternation caused by this incident resulted in a special enquiry by the House of Commons Committee of Privileges. The rising tide of public opinion on this issue, made some MPs sever their relationships with political consultancies. It is not likely that the Committee of Privileges will recommend any radical changes to current procedures, as the practice of MPs undertaking external and paid consultancies outside Westminster is widespread and not illegal.

A useful role

There is a view that MPs are inundated daily with volumes of mail from numerous pressure groups that they don't want and haven't time to read. Many parliamentarians will admit privately this mail is filed immediately in the wastepaper bin. However, there is another side to this story. Parliamentarians in both Houses of Parliament in the UK are poorly resourced, comparatively speaking. Office accommodation, when available at Westminster, is often appalling. Expenses for secretarial and research facilities and for the costs of running a constituency office are better than in former times but are still not generous. MPs in particular look enviously at better paid, vastly better resourced counterparts in the USA and Europe.

At the same time, the volume and complexity of legislation handled at Westminster and Brussels grows apace. Overworked and understaffed, MPs find it difficult to keep themselves briefed and up to date on all the issues of concern to them. In particular, membership of a Standing Committee, which scrutinizes bills clause by clause and line by line, places a very heavy burden on MPs, who, very often, will not be familiar with the detailed technicalities of the subject of legislation. In such circumstances parliamentarians frequently turn for advice and briefing to public affairs and policy specialists often working in-house or for trade associations. These are professionals who are known to be expert in their field, whether it be transport, environment, health or a number of other special subjects.

Parliamentarians respect professionals who are authoritative sources in their field. In addition, they often seek briefing from opposing parties in a public policy issue to ensure they get a rounded picture. These public affairs experts will testify to the fact that MPs beat a path to their door for briefings. The public affairs staff are happy to provide an unpaid research facility for a number of MPs and peers who command respect in the House and who, if they use the briefing material provided by the public affairs manager (and that is not always the case) will do credit to the argument.

Far from offering financial inducement to these MPs to table parliamentary questions or to sign Early Day motions, public affairs managers find it difficult to comply fully with the demands for briefing made on them by various MPs. The lesson is that creditable sources of expertise will be tapped regularly by parliamentarians anxious to make their mark and so progress their careers.

Senator James A McClure, a Republican representing Idaho, has been quoted as saying, 'I personally believe lobbyists have a very useful role. If you want to find out the real information, if you want a breadth of opinion, call the lobbyists who are for it and the lobbyists against it. You will get an education in a hurry. They will give you all the best arguments on both sides. I think the system works'.

Parliamentarian consultants

In addition to retaining a MP or peer, some large corporations and trade associations employ political consultants. As a result we have seen the growth in recent years of the 'political expert' – someone versed in all the arcane customs and practices of the British Parliament and Civil Service. Given the Byzantine labyrinths of some parliamentary procedures, which can remain a mystery even to active members of parliament, there is no doubt that there is a legitimate role for parliamentary consultants. For in-house public affairs managers, the trick is to know when and how to use the services of these consultants. The general consensus is that the consultant should *advise* but the client must *dispose*, and, above all, the client must personally put his or her own case – whether to a civil servant, minister or parliamentarian.

Defensive aspects of public affairs

We have seen that public affairs managers undertake a number of activities. These include *defensive* elements to protect the company (and its customers) from attack, as well as *assertive* elements to improve the company's reputation (and commercial success) with both external and internal audiences. It is perhaps the 'community relations' component of public affairs that has developed most rapidly in recent years – to counteract the growing number of environmental and other pressure groups hostile to corporate activities.[8]

Significant forces – political, economic and social – are at work against the corporate community as a whole. There is a suspicion among many individuals and interest/pressure groups that companies make excessive profits and exploit society and the environment. Perhaps the best expression of that view was summed up in the phrase 'the unacceptable face of capitalism'[9] when describing the corporate greed of a large multinational organization in the 1970s. There are clearly negative image problems that can significantly affect an organization's commercial success.

In recent times many organizations have become convinced that these negative aspects cannot be overcome, and credibility and confidence restored, through traditional public relations techniques. Statements of corporate missions and of social concern have started to make a noticeable appearance in the corporate community. As understanding of the relationship between business and society has increased, so corporate responsibility (also known as enlightened self-interest) has come of age.

Thornton Bradshaw, the Chairman of Atlantic Richfield, has best summed up the mood of business to corporate social responsibility:

The basic goal of private enterprise remains what it has always been – to produce needed goods and services, earn a fair return on investment, and succeed as an economic institution. But the new dimension that must be observed – a new bottom line for business really is social approval. Without it, economic victory would be Pyrrhic indeed ... in the end, all that can really be regarded as certain and unchanging is that a corporation in its day-to-day operations must be sensitive to the public interest. A socially accountable corporation must be a 'thoughtful' institution, able to rise above immediate economic interest and to anticipate the impact of its actions on all individuals and groups, from shareholders and employees to customers, to fellow breathers of the air and fellow sharers of the land. A successful business organization must possess a moral sense as well as an economic sense'.[10]

This concept of enhanced corporate interaction with the social environment has greatly expanded the duties and responsibilities of public relations practitioners and enlarged the scope of the public affairs function.

Assertive elements of public affairs

Support for the organization has to be won and rewon. How do organizations win respect and convince customers to join/continue to support it? Performance is part of the answer: people will go back to organizations that have proved themselves and their products and services to be reliable.

But there is more to winning and maintaining customer loyalty than corporate performance. The most worthy company can find itself without support at times of crises because it has failed to build and sustain important relationships

Public affairs may also be supportive and complementary to marketing. The communication skills used in public affairs may be drawn on directly by marketing to support product promotion. Relationships with government, the media or with pressure groups can be managed so as to create a favourable environment for marketing activities and improve the likelihood that these activities will be successful.

The role of public relations in promotional activities and as an aid to customer relations is stressed by Kotler.[11] He maintains that marketing has become mega-marketing, which he describes as 'the application of economic, psychological, political and public relations skills to gain the cooperation of a number of parties in order to enter or to operate successfully in given markets'.

The marketing approach has limitations. Its critics ask why, if marketing is supposed to increase an organization's sensitivity to the market place, the years of marketing prominence have also seen a growth in consumerism and the bonding together of consumers in organizations such as the Consumers Association to protect their interests? While public affairs can and should complement marketing (and marketing communication in particular), they must also be a *corrective* to the marketing approach, because the perspective on which the former practice is based is broader than marketing perspectives.

Public affairs can raise questions that the marketing approach, with its focus on the market products, distribution channels and customers, and its orientation towards growth and consumption, cannot. Public affairs concerns, as we have seen, are with the relation of groups, one to another, and with the interplay of conflicting and competing interests in social relationships. They are concerned with the reputation of the organization and seek to ensure that its reputation is not threatened by questions about the integrity of its services and activities.

Public affairs has to do with managed communication, and some of the techniques it uses are similar to those used in marketing communication. In marketing, approaches are made to the media in order to generate publicity for products and services. Media relations are also central to public affairs.

In advertising, the publicity message can be completely controlled. However, in public relations tests have shown that editorial messages have more credibility with the reader to a factor of three times or more. This is because the editorial has the authority of the publication or broadcast station, while advertising is clearly seen to be a paid for message.

Advertising is vital to developing brand awareness. However, at some point the law of diminishing returns begins to apply. With large advertising budgets, this means that an extra 10 per cent spent on public affairs is likely to be more effective than the same sum expended on increasing the advertising volume. Public affairs defy the law of diminishing returns.

The British political scene

We have discussed definitions of public relations and where public affairs fit in. We have also looked at the tasks public affairs managers undertake. However, public affairs practitioners do not operate in a vacuum. The political climate in which they operate will not just affect but can fundamentally determine the very nature of the public affairs agenda. It is that political and social climate we must address if we are to understand the changing nature of the role of public affairs practice.

Privatization

The Conservative Party has been the party of government (without a break in office) since 1979. On coming into office, it set itself the task, under Margaret Thatcher, the then Prime Minister, to roll back the frontiers of socialism and state ownership of public utilities, and it has largely succeeded.

Ownership of gas, water, electricity and British Telecom (and to some extent railways and bus companies) is now in private hands, and the nation has become a 'share-owning democracy' in Mrs Thatcher's words. The British Government is considering, or is reputed to have under consideration, the privatization of the Post Office, the Forestry Commission and the coalmines. Even the Civil Service has come in for a measure of privatization via the 'Next steps' initiative, which has resulted in the setting up of Executive Agencies, such as the Highway Agency and the Driver and Licensing Agency, to name but two.

Mrs Thatcher's successor, John Major, initiated the concept of published performance standards for the public service and launched the 'Citizens' Charter' initiative. Citizens now have the right to know what level of service they are entitled to expect of whatever department they are using – whether it is the Inland Revenue or the Department of Education. In addition, in certain circumstances citizens are now able to make a claim for an agreed amount of compensation when the service provided falls below agreed performance levels – as in the case of British Rail's trains running behind the published schedule.

'Glasnost' breaks out

Another development in Mr Major's term of office has been the declared policy of 'open government' or 'glasnost'. It was Michal Gorbachev, President of the former USSR (and the communist leader Mrs Thatcher said she could do business with), who introduced open government in the former USSR and gave the world the term 'glasnost'. (It is often argued that this concept helped to undermine Gorbachev's authority and eventually facilitated his downfall). Mr Major's policy of open government has significant implications for the Civil Service. The decision to publish details of the British intelligence services and their head, Mrs Rimington, would have been unthinkable during the Cold War.

The intention behind the reforms is that the size of the Civil Service should be reduced and it should concentrate on policy processes. Many operational activities have been hived off into executive agencies, leaving a small cadre of policy professionals in Whitehall. Senior civil servants are also being invited to join boards of directors of numerous private enterprises in a non-executive director capacity. So the concept of the remote civil servant, ignorant of the 'real' world of industry and commerce, is diminishing. But with that goes worry about the independence and objectivity of the service.

There is some pressure to introduce into British Government the American tradition of government ministers being able to select, appoint and sack their own officials. Civil servants themselves via their trade union, known as the First Division, are increasingly concerned about the politicalization of their role. Sir Peter Kemp seems to believe that these fears are exaggerated: 'Under the guise of unnecessary fear about so-called "politicalisation", does not anyone recognise how politicalised the Civil Service already is'.[12]

For the public affairs manager attempting to operate in this rapidly changing public arena, several metaphors seem apt. He/she is trying to navigate on a sea with shifting sandbanks. Other public affairs staff comment that some changes in the political scene do not so much constitute a displacement of the goalposts as the removal of the goalposts altogether. Gamekeepers would seem to have become poachers in certain respects and some former poachers are now acclaimed champions of the consumer's right to unregulated economic activity and free enterprise.

Various terms in common parlance in the public policy field have taken on an entirely new meaning. Public transport, for example, is no longer what the name implies – a state monopoly owned and operated by public sector workers. Public transport is *used* by the public but ceased to be owned by them following the deregulation of the buses, the partial privatization of British Rail, the disposal of the public interest in British Airways and now the proposed privatization of the Civil Aviation Authority. The public highway, our roads, are currently one of the last big major utilities in public ownership. The job of the public affairs manager in the years ahead will have somewhat less to do with interaction with the Civil Service and more to do with what are called 'business-to-business' opportunities. Everyone in the public affairs arena will fall into the category of a purchaser or provider of goods and services, and relationships will evolve around such basic concepts as these.

Former civil servants, trained to be paragons of impartiality, independence and integrity, are now expected to be dashing entrepreneurs in the new executive agencies – totally dedicated to customer-driven quality at all (or virtually all) costs. There is a view that transplanting former civil servants, lock stock and barrel, into market-oriented executive agencies will simply result in more of the same in terms of ethos, culture and drive for these agencies – that little will change and that the overall result will simply be to produce more quangos. As Shakespeare said, 'A rose by any other name...'

Faith in some of the old certainties in the public policy arena has been shaken recently. The Ponting Case, the Spy Catcher episode and the Matrix Churchill affair have forced a reappraisal of the traditional belief in fair play and honest dealing at the higher echelons of public life. The admission, in court, under oath, by a former head of the Civil Service that he had been 'economical with the truth', and the allegations that government ministers had endeavoured to withhold evidence from a court of law are hardly likely to inspire confidence in our public servants.[13]

The public affairs manager is therefore faced with new and very real challenges with regard to two of our key publics – parliamentarians and civil servants.

Ethical guidelines

The Public Affairs Council, a Washington based organization of public affairs executives for major US corporations has developed ethical guidelines for business public affairs professionals. These guidelines represent a clear steer for public affairs managers confronted with ethical dilemmas and are outlined below:[14]

A The Public Affairs Professional maintains professional relationships based on honesty and reliable information and therefore:

    1 Represents accurately his or her organization's policies on economic and political matters to government, employees, shareholders, community interests and others.

    2 Serves always as a source of reliable information, discussing the varied aspects of complex public issues within the context and constraints of the advocacy role.

    3 Recognizes diverse viewpoints within the public policy process, knowing that disagreement on issues is both inevitable and healthy.

B The Public Affairs Professional seeks to protect the integrity of the public policy process and the political system, and therefore:

    1 Publicly acknowledges his or her role as a legitimate participant in the public process and discloses whatever work-related information the law requires.

    2 Knows, respects and abides by federal and state laws that apply to lobbying and related public affairs activities.

    3 Knows and respects the laws governing campaign finance and other political activities, and abides by the letter and intent of those laws.

C The Public Affairs Professional understands the interrelation of business interests with the larger public interests, and therefore:

    1 Endeavours to ensure that responsible and diverse external interests and views concerning the needs of society are considered within the corporate decision-making process.

    2 Bears the responsibility for management review of public policies which may bring corporate interests into conflict with other interests.

    3 Acknowledges dual obligations – to advocate the interests of his or her employer, and to preserve the openness and integrity of the democratic process.

    4 Presents to his or her employer an accurate assessment of the political and social realities that may affect corporate operations.

The Chinese salutation 'May you live in interesting times' certainly applies in today's rapidly changing public policy arena, where continuous change seems the only certainty. There is, though, one constant and that is that truth is a precious commodity, 'precious and divine',[15] and to be valued.

The need to cherish that commodity is perhaps even greater in today's multi-media society than it has ever been. Public relations practitioners, whether public affairs managers, or lobbyists, if they are to refute the constant charge of being vehicles for propaganda, must adhere to a clear code of ethics, vigorously enforced by their peer group and profession. Perhaps the best way forward is enshrined in the advice to public relations practitioners from a former press secretary to a presidential candidate: 'You have to be honest, but you don't have to answer every question'.[16]

References

1   Scott M Cutlip, Allen H Center and Glen M Broom, *Effective Public Relations* (6th edition) Prentice Hall.
2   *Ibid.*
3   Jon White (1991) *How to Understand and Manage Public Relations*, Business Books.
4   Keith MacMillan (1991) *The Management of European Public Affairs*, ECPA No 1.
5   Jon White (1991) *op cit.*
6   Philip Kotler (1988) *Marketing Management*, Prentice Hall.
7   Sir Peter Kemp (1994) Remarks to the Research Workshop on the Management of Public Affairs. Templeton College, Oxford.
8   Scott M Cutlip, Allan H Center and Glen M Broom (1985 edition) *Effective Public Relations*, Prentice-Hall.
9   Prime Minister Edward Heath, MP, speaking of Lonrho's activities, 1973.
10 Dennis L Wilcox, Philip H Ault, Warren K Agee (1989), second edition *Public Relations Strategies and Tactics*, Harper & Row.
11 Philip Kotler and William Mindak (1978), Marketing and Public Relations, *Journal of Marketing*, October; and Philip Kotler (1986), Megamarketing, *Harvard Business Review*, Vol. 64, No 2.
12 Sir Peter Kemp (1994) *op. cit.*
13 Dennis L Wilcox, Philip H Ault and Warren K Agee (1989) *op. cit.*
14 *Ibid.*
15 Samuel Butler (1612–1680) *Hudibras.*
16 Kathy Buskin, Press Secretary to Gary Hart, Presidential Election Candidate, 1984.

5

Public relations and marketing

Danny Moss

The relationship between public relations and marketing has always been a somewhat ambiguous and controversial one. Practitioners and academics of both disciplines have continued to argue over where the dividing line between the two disciplines should be drawn. Despite the efforts of both practitioners and academics to resolve the 'territorial boundaries' between the two disciplines, there is still little consensus about where, or for that matter whether, a dividing line should be drawn between marketing and public relations. For some practitioners and academics, in particular, determining the boundaries between the two disciplines has continued to be an issue of prime concern. However, others have argued that the debate over boundaries is rather futile, and that what really matters is not whether a particular set of techniques should be labelled public relations or marketing, but whether they are effective in achieving a firm's desired objectives.

Formal definitions of public relations, such as that offered by the Institute of Public Relations (IPR), emphasize the aim of public relations is that of creating 'mutual understanding and goodwill between organisations and their publics'. While most firms would undoubtedly agree that maintaining goodwill, particularly with customers, is important, they are clearly not concerned with creating and maintaining goodwill for its own sake, but only as a means to an end – that of achieving their business goals. For marketers the primary concern is usually that of maintaining and improving sales and market share, and hence public relations activities designed to maintain goodwill are valued only in so far as they contribute to achieving these objectives.

The 'turf war' between marketing and public relations practitioners has not, however, been fought across the full spectrum of marketing or public relations activities. Few public relations practitioners would argue that pricing or distribution decisions should be their responsibility (although advice about their implications might well be); similarly, few, if any, marketers would lay claim to responsibility for corporate identity design or internal communications. Rather this turf war has focused primarily on the area of market-related communications – the promotional function of marketing and what amounts to the publicity function of public relations.

From a marketing perspective all such promotional activity is viewed as a form of marketing communications (as part of the marketing communications mix) and should therefore come under marketing's control. From a public relations perspective techniques such as product publicity, trade promotions, product editorial, events, and even sponsorship, are seen as essentially specialist public relations techniques that should be handled by experienced public relations practitioners.

Five models of the relationship between marketing and public relations

Philip Kotler, one of the leading marketing academics, has continued to advocate the view that public relations, while a distinct function, should be managed as part of a company's marketing function. In a paper written in 1978 Kotler and Mindak[1] identified five different conceptual models of the relationship between marketing and public relations (see Figure 5.1).

1   Separate but equal functions

This is the traditional view, that the two functions are different in both their perspectives and roles. Marketing exists to identify and meet customer needs at a profit. Public relations serves to create and maintain goodwill towards a company from its various publics in order to enable it to achieve its goals.

2   Equal but overlapping functions

This view is that while marketing and public relations are important and separate functions, they share some common ground. Here areas such as product publicity and customer relations form the most obvious areas of common interest. From this perspective public relations is also seen to serve as something of a counter-balance to the policies of marketing departments, advising marketers on the potentially wider social impact and possible public reaction to their policies.

3   Marketing as the dominant function

This model reflects the view that the public relations function exists essentially to serve the needs of the marketing function – to facilitate the marketing of a

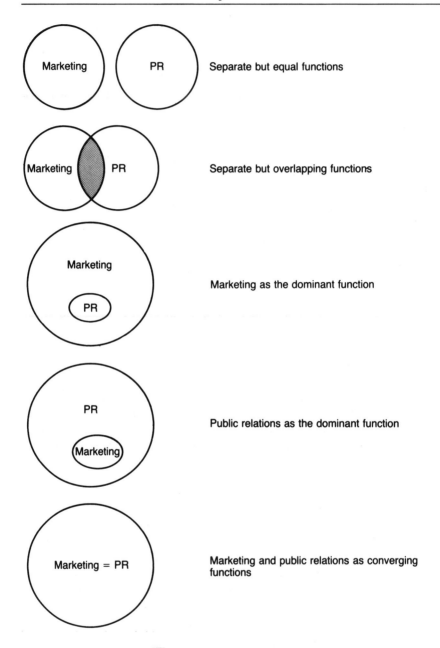

Figure 5.1 *Five alternative models of the relationship between the public relations and marketing functions. (From Kotler and Mindak, see References)*

company's goods or services. This view seems to reject the idea that public relations should exist to help balance the interests of an organization and its publics. It is thus a one-sided orientation in which the organization's interests must come before consideration of any greater 'social good'.

4 Public relations as the dominant function

Although undoubtedly a minority view, it is possible that in some cases marketing might be viewed as a sub-function of public relations. Here the argument is that the prosperity and even survival of a firm depend critically on how it is viewed by its key stakeholder publics – not only customers but also employees, shareholders, communities, government, etc. Satisfying customers, the task of marketing, is only one of a firm's tasks and must be balanced against the needs of these other groups. Thus from this perspective marketing should be placed under the control of public relations to ensure the goodwill of all stakeholders is maintained.

5 Marketing and public relations as converging functions

Perhaps the most controversial of the five models views marketing and public relations as two functions whose concepts and methodologies are rapidly converging. This view recognizes that the two functions are both concerned to some degree with publics and markets, recognizes the need for segmentation, and acknowledges the importance of understanding and influencing attitudes, perceptions, and images in formulating their programmes.

Kotler argues that this fifth model could offer a solution to the inter-departmental rivalries between the two functions, synthesizing the activities of the two functions and reducing conflict and lack of coordination. Moreover, Kotler argues that the divisions between the two functions is already showing signs of breaking down, and closer integration between the two functions is likely to become increasingly common.

Looking at the way the relationship between the two functions is perceived today, some sixteen years after Kotler and Mindak's article was published, one can only conclude that there is little sign of the rivalry between practitioners and academics of the two disciplines diminishing. Why is this the case? One obvious answer is the contentious issue of how power and responsibility should be shared between the two functions. Marketers may have come to recognize the value of public relations to a far greater extent, but accepting that public relations should be treated on an equal footing with marketing in the boardroom is another question altogether.

There is little doubt that marketing has been far more successful in establishing itself as an important management function than has public relations. This partially stems from the fact that marketing has been more widely taught in business schools, and, as a result, managers have a better understanding of marketing concepts. Marketing is also viewed as a far more precise practice, the results of which are capable of being measured more accurately. Marketers have been able to use research to measure and relate changes in a relatively small number of variables such as price, advertising spend, and sales promotion activity to changes in other variables such as sales and market share. Because public relations deals with a larger number of variables, many of which are difficult to measure precisely, such as peoples' attitudes and opinions, it has proved more difficult for public relations practitioners to provide management with accurate measures of the effectiveness of their campaigns. The problems of measurement have not of course been due entirely to the relatively large number and complex nature of variables with which public relations may be concerned. To a large extent the problem has resulted from a lack of research expertise within the profession as well as a reluctance to commit resources to research.

How do marketing and public relations differ?

Because most business managers have had little or no training in public relations, it is perhaps hardly surprising to find that they tend to have only a limited understanding of the full scope of public relations work and tend to see it as primarily a publicity function. As such, public relations is often treated as little more than a subset of the marketing function (as Kotler and Mindak's model of 'marketing as the dominant function'). While most public relations practitioners and academics might deplore this situation, there is little doubt that public relations can and does play an important complementary role alongside traditional marketing activities, and in this context both functions make use of very similar processes and techniques. Both functions are concerned with handling organizational relationships, but the major difference lies in the outcomes they seek to achieve.

While marketing is concerned with promoting exchange relationships with customers and attempts to attract and satisfy customers on a sustained basis in order to achieve an organization's economic objectives, public relations' goal is to attain and maintain accord with other social groupings upon whose support an organization depends to achieve its mission.

Jon White (1991), visiting Professor at City University Business School, suggests that public relations can serve as both as supportive and as corrective function to marketing.[2] In the first of these two roles public relations can assist an organization to achieve its marketing objectives, complementing mainstream marketing activities such as advertising, sales promotion, or sales force activities by helping to promote and strengthen relationships with target customer audiences. As a corrective to marketing, public relations provides another perspective on management decisions, helping management to balance economic considerations against their possible wider social implications. In this latter role public relations is concerned with maintaining the longer-term health of an organization's relationships with all its stakeholders and not just its customer publics. Examining these dual roles of public relations will help shed further light on how the marketing–public relations relationship should be understood.

Public relations support for marketing activities

As a support function for marketing, public relations operates primarily as a publicity function, helping to extend the reach of the marketing budget, complementing the use of advertising and other marketing communications techniques. In consumer markets, in particular, marketing strategies are often concerned with developing or building brands or maintaining customer brand loyalty.

Here advertising has tended to be the principal tool used to communicate brand values and to induce customer trial and repeat purchase. However, the power of advertising to influence consumer purchasing behaviour came under increasing pressure throughout the 1980s and early 1990s as consumers became more sophisticated in the way they viewed and responded to advertising messages. The increasing costs of media space and airtime, the increased fragmentation of media audiences, and the intensification of competition for the attention of audiences, have all contributed to an increasing realization that advertising alone can no longer be relied upon to deliver the results that appeared possible during the 1960s and 1970s. The belief in the effectiveness of advertising to generate brand awareness and loyalty was predicated on the existence of relatively large homogeneous audiences that could be reached relatively cost-effectively via the use of mass media advertising. The growing fragmentation of society, and hence of consumer markets, into many special interest and ethnic groupings, the arrival of video recorders, and changing working patterns and life-styles have all contributed to a vastly different consumer market place compared to that facing firms during the 1960s and 1970s.

As a result of these changes in the consumer market place, many firms have been forced to re-examine the basis of many of their marketing strategies and, in particular, their traditional reliance on mass media advertising. This has led to a move towards more narrowly targeted and focused marketing strategies, requiring a shift away from a heavy reliance on advertising to the adoption of multi-channel communication strategies employing direct marketing, public relations, sponsorship, and sales promotion to a far greater degree than might have been the case in the past. This move towards what has been termed 'integrated marketing communications' will be discussed further later in this chapter.

Where is public relations most effective?

Speaking at the annual conference of the Public Relations Society of America in 1989, Daniel Edelman, head of one of the world's largest public relations consultancies, identified a number of situations in which public relations is likely to prove most effective in supporting marketing objectives:

- With revolutionary break-through type products – those that can make the news.
- Where the company is small and there is little money available for advertising.
- Where television advertising is unavailable through regulatory reasons, e.g. in the case of alcoholic spirits.
- Where there is a hostile environment towards a product or company that has to be turned around, e.g. the problems faced by British Sugar in promoting its products in the face of the strong trend towards greater healthier eating life-styles.

Edelman suggested that public relations tends to be more effective than advertising when:

- Generating new excitement about existing products.
- A company is having difficulties in distributing a product.
- Advertising is well-liked but is failing to build brand recognition.
- A product is relatively complex and takes time to explain.
- Regulations make it impossible to advertise a product.
- When established products or companies are aligned with a cause.

Some examples of where public relations techniques can prove particularly helpful in achieving marketing objectives will help to illustrate how the two functions can work together.

Books

Publishers have long recognized that the success of any new title will often depend upon the type of book reviews it receives in the national and literary press. However, only a minority of all the books published each year can expect to be reviewed in the press and there is no guarantee that they will receive a favourable review. More to the point, many subsequent bestsellers have received far from favourable reviews within the literary columns. Publishers nowadays have recognized the power of good marketing and public relations in promoting their new titles and have become far more proactive in promoting both established and new authors. They have realized that one of the best ways to turn a book into a bestseller is to get the author on to broadcast chat shows, where they are able to publicize their work to a relatively large audience. Equally publishers have recognized the value of organizing 'road shows' for authors to visit bookstores around the country, often linking such tours to local radio and/or television interviews. The phenomenal success of the recent books written by authors such as Jilly Cooper and Jeffrey Archer owes a good deal to a well-organized campaign of television interviews and book-signing tours run by public relations staff.

Fashion

The fashion industry is a notoriously fickle and ephemeral business in which today's highly fashionable design may be discarded almost overnight. At the *haute couture* end of the business publicity and favourable comment by the leading fashion editors is critical to the success of any collection. Public relations rather than traditional marketing techniques clearly play a critical role in keeping any designer in the fashion media 'spotlight' and stimulating interest among potential customers.

Food

Generating food publicity is another area in which public relations has always played an important role. The production of enticing recipes, and the generation of product editorial in food magazines and in the cookery columns of the national press, have long been the staple approaches in promoting new and existing food products.

Motor cars

While most manufacturers engage in extensive advertising campaigns to support the launch of new models, they have recognized the importance of gaining favourable third-party endorsement for their products from the motoring correspondents working for the national and specialist motoring press as well as for the increasing number of broadcast motoring programmes. Arranging test drives for journalists and providing them with background information about new models is one of the key ways in which public relations supports the marketing effort. Public relations is also used to support local dealer networks through the creation of competitions, dealer newsletters, and through generating local media editorial.

While these are only a few of the many areas in which public relations plays an important support role to marketing, they illustrate the potential benefits that can result from the integration of marketing and public relations strategies.

The multiplier effect

Finding ways to maximize the return on the promotional spend has always been a priority for marketers. The rising costs of mass media advertising in recent years has made this an even greater concern. As a result, firms have increasingly looked to public relations to help stretch the degree of media exposure gained by their paid for campaigns, thus multiplying the impact of each pound/dollar spent. Haagen-Daz and Benetton are recent examples of companies that have been particularly successful in generating considerable media coverage for their controversial advertising campaigns. In both cases the degree of media comment their respective advertising campaigns attracted undoubtedly added greatly to consumer awareness of them and hence to their impact.

While the advertising campaigns adopted by these two companies were perhaps not designed specifically with a view to the possibility of generating editorial coverage, nevertheless they do seem to be indicative of a greater awareness on the part of marketers and public relations people of the potential to generate media coverage on the back of a controversial or intriguing advertising campaign. A further example of this linking of advertising and public relations campaigns can be seen in the recent advertising 'battle' between Pepsi-Cola and Coca-Cola for supremacy in the huge worldwide cola market. It was estimated that the equivalent of some $12 million of additional media coverage was generated on the back of Pepsi-Cola's high-profile advertising campaign using celebrities such as Michael Jackson and Madonna.

Of course this link between advertising and public relations is far from typical, and is not something that most companies would be able, or perhaps in some cases would want, to develop. Other opportunities to integrate public relations techniques with marketing activities abound,

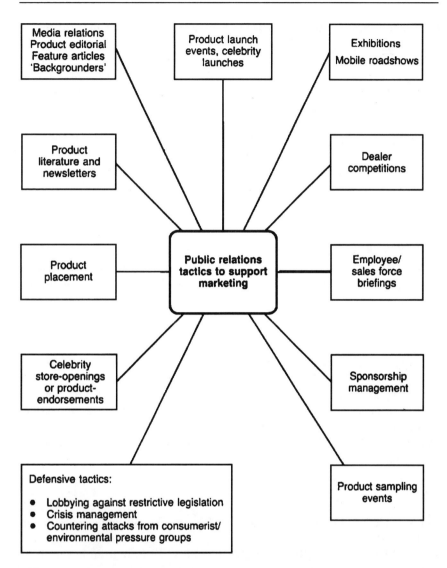

Figure 5.2 *The range of possible public relations tactics to support the marketing function*

providing that firms have the commitment and resources to exploit them. A summary of some of the more common public relations techniques that can be used to support marketing strategies is shown below (see also Figure 5.2).

Public relations techniques that can be used to support marketing

New product launches

- EXCLUSIVE PRODUCT PRESENTATIONS: to selected editors.
- 'TEASER' MAILING TO EDITORS: leaking part of the story, before the main announcement.
- PRODUCT DEMONSTRATIONS: to invited journalists.
- PRODUCT LITERATURE: offered separately, after the main launch for distribution via 'literature available' sections of magazines.
- SALES SUCCESS STORIES: a round up of sales successes after perhaps six or twelve months or on the sale of 1000th product, etc.

Market education

- SPONSORED EDUCATIONAL MATERIAL: a company produces booklets, posters, wall charts, etc., with a high information content to support the use of its products or with a view to building a future market.
- SPONSORED BOOK: as above, but such books may be sold through normal retail outlets.
- PUBLIC DISPLAYS: informational displays provided for use in public places, e.g. in libraries, or cinema lobbies, dealing with a topic of interest to the public as well as relevant to the company's products.
- CUSTOMER GIFTS: a company provides customers with gifts having long-term potential use, e.g. paperweights, notecases, pens, etc., that bear the company/product name.
- POSTAL FRANKING: company correspondence is franked with an informational message.

Feature techniques

- EXCLUSIVE BY-LINE FEATURE: in key non-competing journals, under the name of a company executive.
- EXCLUSIVE MULTIPLE INTERVIEW FEATURE: written in the third person, including references to one's own company alongside other non-competing companies.
- EXCLUSIVE THIRD PERSON FEATURE: written in the third person as if by the journalist him/herself but referring to one company only.
- EXCLUSIVE EDITORIAL VISIT: meeting on a chosen theme between one editor and a key company person.
- GENERAL SYNDICATED FEATURE: one article released without prior negotiation to several journalists for use at their discretion.

- ANGLED SYNDICATED FEATURE: as above, but each feature angled specially to the local area or market concerned, so improving the chance of use.
- PRESS BRIEFING KIT: a folder of company and product releases, material, illustrations, etc., which is distributed to the media to be filed for use when required.
- ADVERTORIAL FEATURE: written in editorial form but placed as a paid-for advertising deal, often in association with a display advertisement.

Press meetings

- PRESS RECEPTION: to announce a new product or service that requires face-to-face demonstration.
- PRESS CONFERENCE: as above, but usually to announce and take questions on an important company news story.
- PRESS BRIEFING: to acquaint journalists with background information for feature use – where immediate coverage is not the prime objective.
- FACILITY VISIT: a planned company tour by a group of invited journalists.

Exhibitions

- EDITORIAL STAND VISIT: advance invitations sent to journalists to visit the company's stand.
- PRESS ROOM KITS: release material placed in an exhibition's press room.
- EXHIBITION NEWSPAPER: company news and feature material supplied for an exhibition's own newspaper.

Editorial product merchandising

- COMPETITIONS: prizes in the form of merchandise supplied to a magazine for offer to readers in return for editorial space.
- PRODUCT MERCHANDISING: products or services (not normally available through retail outlets) are offered to readers at a special price by exclusive arrangement with the supplier company.
- PRODUCT SAMPLES: a sample of the product is delivered to journalists for trial in the expectation of subsequent review in new product features columns.
- READER SAMPLING OFFER: an exclusive editorial deal that offers readers of a publication the opportunity to write in for a free or low-priced product sample – often used in advance of a national launch or as a stimulus to purchase.

Broadcast techniques

' • NEWS INTERVIEW: a solus studio or telephone interview with a company spokesperson on a theme of public interest.
• SYNDICATED PRE-RECORDED CASSETTE: a news or feature interview professionally prepared and issued often with cue sheets by a company to local radio stations for use at their discretion.
• PHONE-IN PROGRAMME: a company initiates a topic of public interest and provides a spokesperson to answer listeners' live questions.

Created events

• AD-HOC SURVEYS: the company carries out an original survey into opinion or practice concerned with some relevant aspect of its industry or market and releases the findings.
• AWARDS SCHEME: a company honours an individual or organization for outstanding achievement in a relevant field.
• MEDIA EVENT: a 'stunt' designed to create a photo-opportunity for the media picture editors, who are notified of the event in advance in order to arrange for coverage.
• CHARITY PROMOTION: a company donates product, services, or cash to support a local or national charity and organizes a photo-opportunity at the time of the donation.
• SPONSORSHIP: a company offers to support a sporting, arts, or community activity in the expectation of reaping goodwill and credit for its support.

Customer relations

• SPONSORED SEMINAR: the company imparts genuinely needed information at free or subsidized seminar for its customers or prospects.
• CONFERENCE: as above, but normally a larger event.
• NEWSLETTER: publication containing product and company information of genuine potential interest to customers.
• USER GROUPS: a company assists users of its products to form a mutual interest group where repeat purchase may be reinforced.
• HOSPITALITY EVENTS: customers and prospects are invited to enjoy special company facilities at major sporting or entertainment events.
• PREVIEW SALES EVENTS: customers are invited to participate at a sales event in advance of the general public, often with special discounts on offer.
• HELP LINE: customers and prospects are offered a telephone information service to deal with enquiries and problems concerned with the company's products or services.

The activities listed above are by no means all the public relations techniques that can be employed to support a company's mainstream marketing activities. However, they do represent some of the more commonly used support activities.

Marketing–public relations (MPR)

The term 'marketing–public relations' or MPR has been used increasingly by both marketers and public relations practitioners since the 1980s. The term emerged originally in the USA to refer to the area of public relations work concerned with support for marketing activities. As the term has gained increasing currency, some observers have suggested that MPR should be recognized as a distinctive discipline or function in its own right, separate from other forms of public relations. Those advocating this view have argued that this form of public relations practice has become sufficiently specialized to warrant being treated as distinct from all other forms of public relations dealing with relationships with non-customer publics. Moreover, supporters of the MPR concept have argued that this area of public relations work should be treated as part of the marketing management function.

Needless to say, most public relations practitioners and academics have dismissed such arguments as little more than a further attempt by marketers to 'highjack' an important part of public relations work and place it under marketing's control. While there is no disputing the growing importance of the area of marketing support work, to suggest that this form of the practice should be treated as a separate discipline in its own right appears to be a further case of 'empire-building' by the marketing function. It is significant that the chief advocates of the MPR concept have tended to come from a marketing background. However, the fact that the term marketing–public relations is increasingly used, particularly within the USA, means that public relations practitioners cannot simply dismiss it as a further instance of empire-building by marketers. There seems little doubt that UK practitioners are likely to find their marketing colleagues willing converts to the concept of a marketing-led public relations function.

Integrated marketing communication

Another concept that emerged and gained increasing currency during the late 1980s was 'integrated marketing communications'. The concept of integrated marketing communications is based on the idea of weaving together the various strands of the marketing communications mix into a more cohesive and seamless entity. This is not a new idea, but until recently it has proved extremely difficult to persuade the various communication functions to accept the idea of a single overarching approach to the planning and management of a firm's communications. Critics of the integrated approach have argued that it has amounted to little more than an attempt by advertisers, in particular, to encroach on the traditional territory of public relations, direct marketing and sales promotion. Advocates of the integrated approach have argued that it represents the most logical way to approach the management of a firm's communication strategies. Their arguments focus on the claim that not only does the integrated approach help ensure better cohesion and consistency between the various messages an organization transmits, but it reflects the way in which audiences experience communications – as a flow of information from indistinguishable sources.

While the logic of an integrated approach to managing organizational communications in its various forms is hard to deny, until recently the divisions between the different communications disciplines has proved a major obstacle to putting such an approach into practice. However, increasing competition for client business in recent years has resulted in a growing number of advertising and public relations agencies merging or forming alliances with direct marketing and sales promotion specialists to offer an integrated package of services to clients in an attempt to secure a larger slice of the available business.

Public relations agencies have been perhaps the strongest opponents of the integrated approach, fearing that they would be forced to play second fiddle to the normally dominant advertising function. However, a number of public relations agencies have begun to embrace the integrated communications concept, arguing that public relations rather than advertising is best placed to coordinate the integration of the various strands of the total communication mix. The basis of their arguments has been the fact that public relations people require a broader understanding of all of an organization's publics, rather than simply customer audiences (the principal concern of advertisers), which enables them to take a more holistic view of the impact of the total communication mix. Whether such arguments will prevail is of course open to question, especially given that advertising generally tends to command the lion's share of most communications' budgets.

What in practice does an integrated approach to organizational communications consist of? Essentially it requires the central coordination or organization of all forms of communication undertaken by a company (both market-related as well as corporate communications). To be successful, the implementation of integrated communications strategies needs to take place on two fronts – ensuring the development of consistent and mutually supporting message strategies, and coordinating the transmission of messages through the various channels used. Clearly if an organization's communications strategy is to achieve the appearance of a 'seamless entity', it is essential that those managing its implementation understand how the total mix of communication activities may be perceived by the target audience(s). While in theory there may seem no reason why such an integration of communications cannot be achieved, in practice the traditional separation and specialization of the different communication disciplines has made it extremely difficult to achieve the necessary degree of cooperation between the different communication specialists.

The following example helps to illustrate how an integrated communication campaign can help maximize the impact of an organization's promotional strategy. When British Airways (BA) launched its major promotional drive offering free flights to any destination in the world, the newsworthiness of this offer allowed public relations staff to generate a vast amount of editorial coverage, almost obviating the need for any advertising support. The sales promotion allowed BA to establish a database for future direct mailings, and direct response advertising, including a toll-free telephone number, helped to enhance the customer database further. By coordinating the various strands of its promotional campaign, BA clearly reaped the benefits of each strand reinforcing the others, thus multiplying the impact of the campaign.

The growing recognition of the benefits of an integrated approach to communication planning presents public relations people with both a challenge and opportunity to enhance their position. While advertising is likely to continue to command the dominant share of most promotional budgets, particularly in consumer markets, the value to marketers of a well-organized public relations strategy has undoubtedly gained increasing recognition in recent years. Rather than oppose the move towards integrated campaign planning, public relations people have the opportunity to seize the initiative by promoting the development of coordinated multi-media campaigns that can enhance the impact of organizational communications with consumers and other key target audiences.

Public relations as a corrective to marketing

So far we have focused on the supportive role that public relations can play alongside mainstream marketing activities. However, as was pointed out earlier in this chapter, public relations can also serve as a corrective to the marketing approach. In this mode public relations seek to bring a more balanced perspective to management decision-making, enabling marketing considerations to be weighed against their possible wider consequences for organizational relationships with non-customer publics. For example, the

1980s saw a growing emphasis on 'green issues' throughout the Western world. Environmental pressure groups such as Friends of the Earth emerged as champions of the green cause. Many firms, recognizing this trend, sought to jump on the 'green bandwagon' by launching ranges of 'environmentally friendly products'. The major supermarket groups in the UK sought to exploit the consumers' sensitivity to green issues by positioning themselves as environmentally conscious operators.

The Safeway chain was one of the leaders of this movement and made a particular point of stressing its 'green credentials'. While recognizing the potential opportunities that this green positioning offered, many public relations advisers urged caution on firms in attempting to go too far down the 'green-path'. Such caution proved well-advised as a number of embarrassing press stories appeared highlighting the not-so-environmentally friendly practices of many of the so-called green leaders. The Safeway supermarket chain experienced just such an embarrassing incident when its plans to open a new cold store facility outside Glasgow were exposed as posing a threat to the ozone layer as a result of the CO_2 gas used in the cooling process at the plant. Safeway's embarrassment was compounded by the fact that it had been making a point of promoting itself as a leader in supporting the 'green consumer movement'. Public relations counsel may not have been able to prevent this turn of events, but it might have highlighted the potential for such an incident to have emerged.

The issue of the repeal of the Sunday trading laws was another area in which public relations counsel was able to play an important part in helping retailers to decide how best to handle their stance on the issue. While major DIY retailers such as B&Q and Texas openly flouted the law, justifying their actions by the claim that they were only responding to consumer demand, Marks & Spencer maintained its opposition to breaching the trading laws and refused to open its stores on Sundays despite the potential loss of trade it incurred by this stance. Although Marks & Spencer's decision resulted in a loss of potential Sunday trade, its decision undoubtedly helped reinforce its image as a concerned and socially responsible organization – an image that has helped it to maintain its position as the UK's best-known and most respected brand.

Perrier's decision to withdraw all stocks of its bottled water following the discovery of minor contamination at the source provides another example of how concern for the long-term reputation of a company may outweigh any concern over the impact on short-term profits. Perrier's action, while costly, proved its commitment to serving its customers' best interests and the company emerged from the crisis with its reputation undoubtedly enhanced.

The above examples serve to illustrate how public relations counsel can help managements take a more balanced view of decisions affecting their commercial operations. While such decisions cannot be taken lightly and may have significant implications for company profits, at least in the short term, sometimes short-term considerations may have to be waived in the interest of the longer-term prosperity or even survival of a company. Here public relations people can help bring a wider perspective to bear on important policy decisions that staff concerned primarily with market performance may find more difficult to weigh accurately.

Summary

In this chapter we have highlighted the continued confusion and even animosity that exists between the marketing and public relations functions. Despite the growing recognition of the potential value a company can gain from having an effective public relations function, public relations continue to play 'second fiddle' to the marketing function in many 'fast moving consumer goods' (fmcg) companies in particular. It was suggested that the reason for this situation is probably the lack of understanding and training in public relations among most of today's managers.

It was suggested that the principal area of confusion over marketing–public relations lies in the area of publicity or marketing support activities. Here various conceptual models of the relationship between the two functions were explored. A range of marketing support techniques that public relations can employ were examined and the alternative role of public relations as a corrective to the marketing function was highlighted.

The chapter also examined the emergence of the concepts of marketing–public relations (MPR) and integrated marketing communications. It was suggested that these two emerging concepts are often seen by public relations people as a further attempt by marketing to encroach upon their area of operation. It was suggested, however, that public relations practitioners cannot afford to ignore or dismiss the emergence of these concepts and should seek to take the initiative in promoting a more effective cooperation between the various communications disciplines.

References

1 Kotler, P and Mindak, W (1978) Marketing and public relations: Should they be partners or rivals?, *Journal of Marketing*, October.
2 White, J (1991). *How to understand and manage public relations*. London: Business Books.

6

Public relations in central government

John Cole-Morgan

The operation of a democracy is dependent upon a regular two-way flow of information between government and governed. How to communicate occupies the minds of government ministers and civil servants often as much as policy. There is little point in passing a law or providing a service if no one is made aware of it. And, for example, how does a government explain to a nation living beyond its means that at any time the cake of national wealth is finite and that it has the choice of producing more or consuming less? Such problems faced governments long before the professional services of information specialists became an integral part of the government machine. This chapter therefore looks first at the traditional means of communication and then at the specialist services on which governments can now call for assistance.

The traditional contact between government and governed is through Parliament. When in debates ministers speak on subjects with which their department is concerned – setting out policy, answering criticism and putting forward facts and arguments – the government department is making an effort to establish and maintain mutual understanding between itself and the people of the country, as much as when it issues a press notice.

During Question Time ministers have to stand up to criticism and justify the action of their department. Many of the questions are inspired by press reports or matters brought to MPs' notice by their constituents. Continuous exposure to Parliamentary questions helps to keep departments abreast of the general tide of public opinion, or at least warns them when they are running contrary to it.

Parliament of course is not the sole means of contact with the outside world for a minister. Ministers have ready access to press, radio and television and it is fairly certain that anything newsworthy they say to their constituents, or on a public platform, will be reported. But the Government does not have privileged access to the media; it is the importance and newsworthiness of ministers' statements which are decisive.

From time to time ministers will meet the lobby correspondents. Every important British newspaper and agency has a lobby correspondent and usually a deputy as well. Lobby correspondents have the special privilege of access to the Members Lobby just outside the Chamber of the House of Commons. They therefore have the opportunity of discussing with ministers the political topics of the day. It is the code of lobby correspondents not to reveal the source of information given to them and therefore ministers can provide them with background information, or reveal the way in which they intend to deal with a particular subject. The existence of the lobby greatly eases communications between government departments and the press, especially as lobby correspondents are so easily contacted. However, ministers usually only go to the lobby at the invitation of the Lobby Correspondents Association.

Ministers deal directly with a great number of people. They visit factories, hospitals, schools; they receive deputations and they correspond with members of the public, commercial companies, trade associations, local authorities, etc. In addition, they receive a great many letters from fellow MPs on behalf of constituents and as a result are well placed to assess public opinion and the likely public reaction to government actions.

Ministers are not the only people to make public statements on government matters. Some senior officials make public speeches on non-political subjects on behalf of their ministers, and officials generally write to individual members of the public and appear before Parliamentary Committees and Royal Commissions, as well as maintaining special contact with particular groups on a day-to-day basis.

Each government department has its own special publics. The Department of Education and Science, for example, has four special publics – universities, local education authorities, teachers and parents. In some cases the responsibility for communication with the public is delegated onto QUANGOS, quasi-autonomous non-governmental bodies, such as the British Council, the British Tourist Authority, the British Standards Institution and the British Overseas Trade Board.

A large number of papers are initiated by government departments and laid before Parliament, but there is in addition a great deal of information that comes from government departments which is not laid before Parliament. Much of it is statistical, such as the *Monthly Digest of Statistics* and most of it is printed through Her Majesty's Stationery Office.

The British Government information services

It is now some thirty-five years since, after false starts mainly stimulated by the needs of two world wars, government finally established a recognized interdepartment professional service to effect communications between government and the various publics it serves. Previously the status of press officers in government departments was uncertain, but the increasing and more detailed part played by government in the daily lives of British citizens made it essential that citizens be told of their new rights and of their responsibilities as soon as possible after Parliament has legislated. The increase in the number and complexity of social and economic measures affecting the life of the community and the change in Britain's relations with the world at large coincided with the growth in technical means of disseminating information widely, and quickly made essential the establishment of organized information services, skilled in dealing with how to say what departments wanted to say. At home, the Government information services can supplement news media in explaining legislation and other matters to the public in Britain. Overseas, information work supports the country's diplomatic, economic and commercial aims abroad.

Political neutrality

The information services are staffed by civil servants whose duty it is, as for all civil servants, to explain and further the policies of the Government of the day, regardless of its political complexion. Therefore it has been necessary to ensure that the information services are not used for party political, as distinct from governmental, purposes.

All ministers have a dual position as heads of their departments and also as members of their own political party. The line between the two is not always clear. However, when ministers make speeches, the rule is that the information services only operate on official occasions and publicize their speeches only by issuing a purely factual press statement. When a minister speaks on a party platform, e.g. in a party political broadcast or on a party occasion, publicity will only be given through the party's channels.

During general elections, the official information services suspend most activity, from nomination day to polling, to avoid competing with parliamentary candidates for the public's attention.

At all times the issue of press notices and the selection of papers for press advertising is made on the basis of their effectiveness in reaching the public.

Information officers are not allowed to discuss the merits of government policy with the press or public, although they may repeat to enquirers the declared objectives and ideas of their ministers, e.g. quotes from speeches.

The convention has grown up that the information services give the public, usually through the press and broadcasting media, the background of facts against which proposed legislation can be set. Public money is not normally spent on producing paid publicity about a subject still under parliamentary consideration.

Parliamentary privilege

The contents of Parliamentary Bills, White Papers and other matters that are subject to parliamentary privilege, cannot be anticipated by information officers, but they can, however, arrange for the press to receive information simultaneously with this information being given to Parliament.

Departmental information services

Departmental ministers are responsible to Parliament for the information policy of their department. There is an information division in every major department. The size, structure and title may vary from department to department, but the objectives are similar and the information divisions have similar functions and common problems.

In 1947 the objectives of information divisions were defined as follows:

1 To create and maintain informed opinion about the subjects with which each department deals.
2 To use all methods of publicity, as suitable, to help the department to achieve its purpose.
3 To assist and advise in all matters bearing on relations between the department and its public.
4 To advise the department on the public's reaction to the policies or actions of the department.

The information officers who staff the home departments usually have relevant experience in journalism, publishing, advertising, photography, films, broadcasting, exhibitions, etc. In the Foreign and Commonwealth Office, however, information staff are non-specialist officers of the diplomatic service.

Sir Harold Wilson, writing in the journal of the Institute of Public Relations said: 'The information officer's duty is to give facts, either on his own initiative or more frequently, in response to enquiries from the press or the public. It is not part of his duties to engage in political propaganda, still less to build up the image of any of the ministers of his department'. Information officers therefore provide a service not only to their department

and to their ministers, but to the media. Ministers make their pronounce-
ments to 600 MPs, but they are intended to be understood by the whole
nation. The press and broadcasting media act as intermediaries, but they
need the information at a time and in a form they can use. From their needs
has grown the practice of issuing the embargoed press notice and advance
circulation of publications.

The role of the Chief Information Officer

Chief Information Officers serve their minister as experts in public
relations. With a status usually of assistant secretary (which is a senior
management post) or above, they have direct access to the minister and the
permanent secretary (the chief executive of the department) and attend a
great number of policy-forming meetings held by ministers and senior civil
servants. They are responsible for advising their departments on the public
relations implications of their policies and also they are responsible for the
quality of the press and public relations work done by their division. They
do not formulate policy, but in trying to put it over to others often find
themselves contributing to the shaping of policy. They have three kinds of
duty towards the public:

1   To tell them what government is doing on their behalf and with their
    money.
2   To make them aware of their rights and obligations.
3   To persuade them to do something, e.g. to use condoms as a protection
    against AIDS.

In some departments the information division is expected to draft ministers' speeches. In others they may never see them until they are in the final
form. At press conferences ministers will normally be accompanied by their
chief information officer or a deputy, as well as other senior departmental
officials. Chief Information Officers meet weekly to exchange views and to
sort out the diary of forthcoming events to avoid clashing of dates for important announcements.

Although the information division is there to serve the minister, most of
the Chief Information Officer's time is spent advising Civil Service
colleagues that the information division exists as a service division to the
rest of the department in the same way as a public relations firm operates
on behalf of its clients. The information division therefore receives very
large numbers of internal papers from which it sifts matters that may be of
interest to the public and organizes the release of that information which
can and should be made public.

The information division is the main contact between the department and the press, television and radio. If ministers talk directly to the press, they will normally tell the information division what they said. Most departments have rules on how and when civil servants may talk to the media and civil servants normally consult the information division or ask them to be present when they have any contact with the media.

Usually Chief Information Officers see more of their minister than does any other civil servant, except the Permanent Secretary, in the department and they are therefore required to make their judgement from their own knowledge and evaluation of the policy of the department and their minister's thinking. Chief Information Officers through their press officers are expected to answer questions the press have a right to put to government on matters of fact and to provide guidance on matters of interpretation. It is therefore important that press officers are part of the communications scene and that they are known by journalists. In many departments a duty press officer is available around the clock to answer enquiries.

The organization of the information division

Most information divisions have three sections: press, publicity and briefing. The publicity section deals with paid publicity – everything from press and television advertising to the production of books, posters and films. Publicity directly affects the work of the department by making it easier to administer, e.g. when the general public is called upon to take specific action at a certain time, or by making known the services and benefits available. From time to time the duties of the departmental information staff include the mounting of campaigns aimed directly at the public, e.g. the 'AIDS' campaign mounted by the Department of Health and Social Security and the 'Don't Drink and Drive' campaign mounted by the Department of Transport. In such cases the department would seek the assistance of the Central Office of Information, which would advise the department on advertising methods and brief the agency appointed to handle the campaign, but the responsibility for the campaign still rests with the department's Chief Information Officer on behalf of the minister. Judgement of how things should be told must be the officer's. In most departments the briefing section is concerned with the collection of information and the preparation of briefing and the writing of articles and speeches.

Central Office of Information (COI)

The Central Office of Information is a common service department that produces publicity material on a repayment basis at the request of ministerial departments for use in the United Kingdom and overseas. It has a present staff of about 900, of which nearly half are in the information officer group, most of whom are specialists recruited from the private sector. The COI either creates material itself or arranges for commercial agencies to do so. Press and television advertising campaigns are undertaken by advertising agencies and films are made by film companies under contract.

The COI is headed by its Director-General assisted by the deputy director general. There are four groups: three production groups covering home and overseas work, each headed by a director and each subdivided into specialized services; and in addition there is a client services director, who oversees day-to-day relations with customers.

Advertising

The COI handles government advertising campaigns for most departments. It advises departments on advertising methods, recommends on the cost-effective deployment of funds available, briefs the agency appointed to handle the campaign and monitors the day-to-day work. Recruitment advertising for the armed services, police, nurses, etc., accounts for a large proportion of the total expenditure of more than £100 million a year.

The Advisory Committee on Advertising (ACA) is an independent group of media and marketing professionals appointed by ministers and advises the COI on policy matters, suitable advertising agencies for government work and cost-effective working methods, including ways of selecting and buying media.

Nineteen advertising agencies are currently contracted by COI on behalf of government departments, each selected after consultation with the ACA. ACA-approved advertising agencies are used for centralized media-buying as well as for running campaigns. The committee reviews agency performance annually in the light of departmental and COI appraisals and confirms contracts or suggests revisions. In the past years committee and COI initiatives have led to considerable success through centralized buying for press, television, posters and radio.

Each year additional agencies not currently working on government advertising are nominated by ACA for inspection by the COI, which then provides a confidential report to the committee assessing the agency's potential for future government work.

Home Publications

Home Publications writes, edits, designs and arranges distribution for a wide range of booklets, leaflets and posters throughout the UK explaining the effects of government policy and legislation to many different audiences. A substantial amount of printed recruitment material is produced for the armed and public services.

Printing is arranged through Her Majesty's Staionery Office, which also acts as publisher for titles put on sale.

Up to 3000 publications are produced annually.

Research unit

Although much of the research unit's work relates to advertising, a wide variety of projects concern other areas of government publicity, including print (such as leaflets, information booklets and forms), exhibitions, and films. The purpose is to enhance the cost-effectiveness of the COI's publicity output by means of independent market research. Projects include background research to help understand a target market as well as creative development research and 'evaluation research' to check specific campaigns.

The purpose of evaluative research is often to help determine whether the cost of the campaign was more than offset by the resulting savings, e.g. in reduction in road accidents or fires in the home.

Viewdata

Coordination of government input to the viewdata system is linked with the design and implementation of viewdata data banks for a wide variety of purposes.

Photographic services

A wide variety of photographic services is provided for government departments, other COI services, overseas missions and foreign correspondents. A sales counter supplies crown copyright pictures to the general public on payment of standard fees. The section has its own photographers, photo researchers, darkrooms, and a photographic library that contains a stock of some 300,000 black and white and colour photographs covering most aspects of British life and activities and well-known personalities in every sphere.

Exhibitions

The exhibition service plans, designs and supervises the construction of a large number of exhibitions and displays for government departments in the UK.

Overseas, it deals with exhibitions and displays funded by the Foreign and Commonwealth Office, ranging from modest displays to British participation, often coordinated with other EC countries, in major trade fairs and world expositions. Government support for participation by British companies in overseas trade fairs is the responsibility of the British Overseas Trade Board.

Films and television

The films and television service provides television programmes, films, video tapes and audio-visual presentations for use in Britain and overseas. Most of them are produced or commissioned by the COI, but films are also acquired from other sources and distributed by the COI. Over thirty-five advertising commercials and twenty-five short public service television features for free transmission are produced each year. At any one time some thirty longer documentary films and video tape programmes are in production. Home departments brief COI on their requirements and although it often commissions outside technical services, the COI maintains creative and financial control and is responsible for ensuring that the resulting product fulfils its purpose. It is responsible for a variety of television programmes and documentaries, which receive widespread transmission overseas. The COI is responsible for the provision of facilities for resident television correspondents and teams visiting from overseas.

Overseas press

News items, feature articles, topical commentaries and press pictures are supplied daily by telex or airmail to British missions abroad, mainly for reproduction in local newspapers and periodicals. A special industrial service provides stories about new products, processes, and services and gives publicity support to British participation in exhibitions and trade fairs, at home and abroad. Supplements on particular industries are prepared and placed in leading overseas trade and technical magazines.

Overseas publications and foreign languages

Books, pamphlets, folders and magazines are produced for overseas use and, depending on their destination, may contain material of general interest or specifically in support of exports. The reference services include the annual 'Britain' handbook, the monthly *Survey of Current Affairs*, and a range of titles on individual topics. Photographic display material – posters and captioned picture sets – are also provided. The translation services of the foreign language sections are used by all COI's overseas services.

Radio

Radio items and programmes are supplied by direct line or on tape, for transmission by radio stations overseas, and by local radio stations in the UK. Overseas items are supplied in a total of five languages.

Overseas visitors and information studies

Every year arrangements are made for some 1500 visitors to Britain from more than 100 countries at the request of the Foreign and Commonwealth Office. They include ministers and other leading politicians, journalists, broadcasters and other people of influence officially invited to Britain as guests of the British Government. Help is also given to sponsored visitors who come at their own expense but need help in arranging a programme and making contacts. Visits vary in length from a few days to three or four weeks. Each is individually planned to take account of the needs and wishes of the visitor. Training courses for information officers to overseas governments, and introductory courses for diplomatic service commercial and information personnel, are provided by the information studies unit.

Regional organization

A regional information network is provided by seven COI regional offices in England, the Scottish Information Office, the Welsh Information Office and the Northern Ireland Information Services. These offices, as well as providing a common departmental information service in their regions, are responsible for collecting and supplying material from the regions to COI headquarters for use in the overseas information services and they assist with the arrangements for overseas visitors.

Overseas information services

Just over half of COI staff are employed on overseas services, and export publicity accounts for over half of all overseas work. The objective of the official British information services overseas is to present the facts and Britain's point of view, so that people of other countries have every opportunity of understanding British ideas, policies and objectives. The objectives of commercial publicity are to support Britain's position as a nation dependent on trade (both visible and invisible) by convincing overseas opinion that Britain is a well-integrated industrial country that is stable, skilled, forward-looking and technologically advanced and therefore a sound trading partner.

The methods used to meet the overseas publicity objectives vary with the development of policies, the requirements of overseas posts, the definition of target audiences and the available media; but the main elements of the COI's publicity output, not necessarily in order of priority, are:

1 Information about positive political, social, environmental and particularly economic developments.
2 Publicity for British exporters participating in BOTB-supported joint ventures, trade missions and other events overseas; and publicity for major UK trade fairs.
3 Publicity for new and improved products, processes and services, showing in specific case history terms that British industry is producing the goods that buyers want overseas.
4 Extended publicity for products and services whose excellence is such that they reflect credit on British industry as a whole.
5 Publicity designed to show the achievement and reliability of sectors of British industry and commerce, e.g. aerospace, ceramics, chemicals, North Sea oil, the City of London.
6 Publicity for research and development that shows that British exporters are backed by scientific and technological initiative and follow through of a high order.

The British overseas information services were late to develop and evolved rather haphazardly. The Earl of Drogheda in a summary of a report of an enquiry into the services published in April 1954 said, 'They have always, moreover, been regarded as something of a Cinderella by a people who instinctively dislike the idea of self-advertisement'.

Overseas information policy is set by the Foreign and Commonwealth Office, and guided in commercial matters by the Department of Trade and Industry and the British Overseas Trade Board. The effectiveness of the overseas information service depends in part on the efficiency of the Diplomatic Service officers who staff the information posts in our Embassies, High Commissions and Consulates overseas. These are non-specialists, but are often supported by locally engaged officers with information experience.

In general the British Government does not buy space in overseas media, so it is only possible to obtain press coverage or radio or television time if the material supplied is good enough and meets the publisher's criteria of topicality and relevance. As stated earlier, the COI is responsible for providing feature articles, news items and photographs for the press, films and news material for television, plus line feeds, tapes and scripts for radio, reference documents for selective distribution, and books and magazines for free distribution overseas. It is also responsible for staging exhibitions other than trade and cultural exhibitions, which are the responsibility of the British Overseas Trade Board and the British Council respectively.

Britain's image overseas is also influenced by two other elements – the BBC's external services and the British Council.

BBC external services

The BBC through its external services broadcasts all over the world in English and, at the time of going to press, thirty-six foreign language services for a total of some 732 hours a week. The main objectives are to give unbiased news, to reflect British opinion and to project British life and culture. News bulletins, current affairs programmes, political commentaries and topical magazine programmes form the main part of the output.

The languages in which the external services broadcast and the length of time each language is on the air are prescribed by the Government. Apart from this, the BBC has full responsibility and it is completely independent in determining the content of news and other programmes. The BBC World Service broadcasts for twenty-four hours a day in English, and BBC news bulletins and other programmes are rebroadcast by the domestic radio services of many countries.

The British Council

The British Council is part of Britain's overseas representation. Its aim is to promote overseas an enduring understanding and appreciation of Britain through cultural, educational and technical co-operation. Although funded mainly by the British Government, it is a non-political, independent organization with a Royal Charter. In most countries it works independently of the British Embassy, wherever possible in separate premises. Through its staff in about eighty countries it aims to establish lasting relationships by arranging training and study in Britain; sending British specialists overseas; recruiting British teachers for posts overseas; supplying information about Britain through its 100 or so libraries overseas; teaching the English language; presenting British arts overseas; arranging exchange programmes; and helping to develop links between educational and scientific institutions and twinnings between towns and regions.

Acknowledgements

In preparing this chapter I have drawn widely on a report of the Royal Institute of Public Administration entitled *The Government Explains – A Study of the Information Services*, written by Marjorie Ogilvy-Webb and published by

Allen & Unwin in 1965. I was also guided by a Civil Service College lecture entitled *The Role of the Information Officer*, given by Mr Henry James in 1975, when he was Director General of the Central Office of Information.

Further reading

The student may find it helpful to consult the annual edition of the *Official Handbook on Britain* published by Her Majesty's Stationery Office, the COI reference sheet *British Government Information Service* and the COI booklet *Guide to Overseas Services*. The names and titles of those in Government information work in the UK are published twice yearly in a COI booklet *Public Relations, Information and Press Officers in Government Departments, Public Corporations, etc;*, the names of information officers in Britain's Embassies, Consulates and High Commissions overseas are available from the Diplomatic Service Overseas Reference List available from the Staff Records Section of the Foreign and Commonwealth Office.

Note: The views expressed by the author are his own and should not be interpreted as those of the Department of Trade or the British Council.

7

Public relations in local government

Brian Harvey

Introduction

The Institute of Public Relations defines public relations practice as 'the planned and sustained effort to establish and maintain goodwill and mutual understanding between an organization and its publics'. In broad terms this definition is as much applicable to local government as it is to any other organization: commercial, industrial or governmental. In a sense local government is, by its very nature, a vast public relations exercise. A local authority is run by a group of members or councillors, elected by the public, who in this case are the local residents. Local government officers are employed by the authority and their salaries are paid by the public for whom they work. The elected representatives are answerable to the public and at regular intervals they seek public approval for their policies and actions. If the public do not approve, then the ruling members are literally 'sacked' and new members with new policies take their place.

Thus the framework for establishing and maintaining mutual understanding between 'the organization' and 'the public' already exists, and has done so for a very long time, with the elected member as the focus of communication.

In practice, local authorities vary considerably in the importance they place on professional public relations practice. For example, the number of staff employed can range from a single-person operation to one employing a significant number of staff, and this is reflected in the budget allocated. Much depends on the attitudes prevailing amongst elected members and what importance they place upon the image of their authority, and how they wish to communicate and relate to their public, or, as they are increasingly referred to, their *customers*.

An approach to local government public relations

It is this change in approach from providing services *to* the public, to providing them *for* the customer that has had pronounced effects on the way in which a local authority operates and this has substantially increased the potential impact the public relations function can have. The concept of a local authority having customers is a comparatively new one and one which is still a little alien to some local government officers who see their authority as being the sole provider of service to the public on a strictly 'take it or leave it' basis.

That approach has become increasingly rare, however, and it is now commonplace for customer-care programmes, developed in the private sector, to be adapted and applied to local government in response to the more sophisticated expectations of the modern consumer. Certainly the customers have a right to quality service, whether they are visiting a bank, building society, High Street shop, hospital or Town hall reception desk, and a great deal of effort has gone into making such areas more accessible, welcoming and user-friendly.

Certainly, too, a customer, as a council taxpayer, has the right to expect a quality service in areas such as refuse collection, council house maintenance and leisure and sports facilities. But how can this concept be applied in some aspects of the work of Education and Social Services Departments. Who is the social worker's customer in the extreme situation of having to take a child into local authority care? Is it the child concerned, is it his or her parents, or is it society at large? Similarly, who is a teacher's customer? Is it the child, the parents, further and higher education establishments, employers or again society at large? How does one, in these situations, begin to address the needs of the customer? How does a housing benefits clerk explain to a customer that he or she is not entitled to a particular benefit? In such situations and others where the council has a statutory duty to perform it is not always easy to apply the generally accepted model from the commercial sector of 'the customer as king'.

So who are a local authority's customers? The local residents are obviously a large group. So too are the authority's staff and its elected members. Visitors to the area are a significant group, who can leave with a lasting impression of the service they have received from a local council. Given the importance of economic development and regeneration, clearly industry and commerce from an important group, not only those businesses already operating but also potential new investors who may wish to relocate their business. Other public sector bodies have a special relationship with the council, as do neighbouring local authorities and national government. Voluntary sector groups make significant contributions to the life of the community and they often rely heavily on support from the local authority, as do the vulnerable and disadvantaged of all age groups. Finally, the media are an important customer group, as well as also one of the main channels through which a council can communicate with its other customer groups.

Objectives of the public relations function

A dynamic public relations function is crucial if a council is to communicate effectively with all its different customer groups. One point should be made clear, however: public relations officers work for the council, they do not work for a political party. The policies of the council are established by the current majority party, and it is these policies, once they have entered the administrative machinery and have become council policies, that the public relations officer handles. The political complexion of the majority party may change and the change may bring with it completely new policies. Public relations officers will explain these policies with the same expertise that they used under the previous majority party.

The official viewpoint is the view of the council and, while the press or customers may not like that view, they will at least accept that it is being delivered by an impartial officer and not by someone with a political axe to grind. Within this framework it is possible to identify key objectives which must be met in the operation of a successful public relations function:

1 To establish, maintain and project the authority's corporate character and identity.
2 To create understanding of the policies, procedures and activities of the authority, by keeping customers as fully informed as possible.
3 To respond, where appropriate, to criticism of the authority.
4 To establish and maintain effective channels of public communication available to the authority, and to develop a full range of appropriate techniques.
5 To create and maintain within the authority an awareness of the need to communicate with its various customer groups, and to ensure a sustained level of responsiveness to customer needs and opinions.
6 Generally to manage the authority's public relations function, and to advise on the public relations implications of the policies and activities of the authority and on the formulation of public relations policies.

In successfully meeting these objectives the Public Relations Officer in a modern, forward-thinking and image-conscious local authority has a range of devices and techniques at his or her disposal — exactly the same as those employed by counterparts in the private sector. These opportunities must be grasped with the same degree of energy, enthusiasm and professionalism.

Where it begins

Public relations activity in the town hall or civic centre begins with the fundamental and often overlooked minor matters. It begins at the front door, on the telephone and with correspondence. The pleasantly decorated entrance hall, well-signposted, and with an accessible reception desk that is open at times to suit the customer, creates a positive first impression and makes a major statement about the organization. Trained and knowledgeable receptionists, chosen for their politeness and cheerfulness and perhaps wearing corporate uniforms and definitely wearing name badges, make a lasting impression on the customer and immediately create the feeling that questions will be answered and problems sorted with the minimum of fuss. Telephones answered without delay by staff who are not afraid to give their name and their department suggests right away someone who is prepared to take up an issue and deal with it. Letters answered promptly, personalized to the recipient and signed by the member of staff who wrote it indicate efficiency and ownership of the matter. Particular attention to those groups of customers with special needs, e.g. letters in braille or on audio-tape, reception staff trained in how to 'sign' for deaf customers, demonstrates an authority that cares. Gone for ever are days when a customer should feel that he or she is having to deal with a faceless and inefficient bureaucracy that doesn't care, is unresponsive to their needs and for whom the customer is just a number.

The public relations officer can play a major role not only in the creation and implementation of this customer focus but in the maintenance of standards and attention to detail that is required.

Publications

Local government corporate communications is big business. A recent survey of local authorities indicated that it spends an estimated £250 million and produces some 60,000 items of publicity material each year. Sometimes, sadly, the production of some publications, be they cheap and cheerful leaflets or expensive and glossy brochures, is embarked upon without asking the most fundamental questions. What is its message? Who will read it? Is it purely for information or does it require some subsequent action on the part of the reader? Is it clear what that action is? Is it written in a style and language that will be easily understood? Is it jargon-free? What about those customers for whom English is not their first language or those who have a visual impairment? The list of considerations is endless, and they all have implications for the content, style, design and targeting of the finished publication.

A well thought out message, written in an easy to understand, straight-forward language, and designed in an accessible and attractive format results in a publication that does its job well and at the same time provides a positive corporate image for the authority. And it need not be expensive. Indeed some of the best-received publications have been produced on the proverbial shoestring, while particularly glossy, colourful and expensive productions are sometimes criticized for being extravagant and 'a waste of public money'.

One word of caution about publications. Sometimes as a way of reducing costs associated with the production of publications such as Business Directories, A to Z Guides to Services and Planning Handbooks, a propor-tion of the space is allocated for sale to advertisers. Too much advertising can not only dilute the impact of it being a council publication, but care must be taken to ensure that the council is only associated with advertising that will not compromise it or expose it to adverse publicity.

Many authorities are now producing newspapers or newsletters distributed to every home in their area. Before deciding to produce one, an authority should consider the following:

1 Will it be a first-rate job, comparing favourably with other newspapers residents buy or receive, yet not so lavishly produced that it gives the impression that the public's money is being wasted?
2 Will it be designed to provide answers to questions in people's minds, or to create interest in local government activities that do not interest them at present?
3 If it seeks advertisements, will this antagonize the local newspapers, which could regard it as council-subsidized competition.
4 Will a majority of those who receive it wish to read it or will it be cynically received as a 'council PR exercise'?

After several issues have been produced, some market research on these and other questions would be valuable.

Press, radio and television

Media relations forms a substantial part of public relations work in local government. Around 50 per cent to 70 per cent of local government public relations officers carry out some media relations work, in which an organi-zation establishes and develops a good working relationship with the media, one aimed at achieving mutual understanding. The basic purpose of good media relations is to ensure that a local authority's point of view is accurately and fairly presented in media coverage of its work.

In recent years there has been a vast and rapid increase in the number and range of media outlets. Newspapers, both paid-for and freesheets, maintain healthy circulations. National and local radio stations, both BBC and independent, have loyal and sizeable listening audiences, and the choice of TV channels on both terrestrial and satellite networks is expanding at almost mindboggling speed. Not only is the public faced with a seemingly ever-growing selection but, for media relations purposes, the opportunities to generate coverage are vast. And local government is rising to the challenge. It is now not sufficient for the Public Relations Officer simply to react to media enquiries, an important service though this will continue to be. What he or she has to address now is how to maximize positive coverage for what is happening in his or her council. In other words, what is called for is a proactive strategy.

Local government officers used to be content to keep their good news to themselves, and as a result the many good things happening in local government failed to get the media coverage they deserved. Nowadays the situation has changed and it is now much more usual to identify positive stories about local authority initiatives in both the local and national press. Partly this must be because more resources are being allocated to public relations, partly, too, because the calibre of people working in the field has improved, and because generally there is a growing confidence in a local council's ability to present itself in a positive light. So what are the practical steps that can be taken to generate this kind of positive coverage?

First the Public Relations Officer (or, in some authorities, the more-specialized Media Relations Officer) must keep up to date with what is happening in his or her authority and with what issues are currently being debated. This can be achieved in part by reading all committee papers on a regular basis and by attending committee meetings.

Secondly, it is vital to establish a rapport and understanding with the elected members and to develop a formal and informal network of contacts amongst fellow members of staff. It is these contacts which can generate so many ideas for good stories.

Thirdly, a good professional relationship must be established with the media. This potentially achieves two objectives: more material may be published and, importantly, that which is published is accurate and a fair interpretation of the situation. Paying attention to media deadlines, always getting back to a journalist when you say you will, and targeting stories appropriately, are clearly basic good practice. So too is ensuring that journalists receive all relevant agenda papers for committee meetings. Many authorities also offer other facilities to journalists, such as a press room, with phones, in which to write and send their copy. Larger and more sophisticated authorities sometimes provide rooms for use as radio studios with live broadcasting facilities from council and committee chambers, and closed circuit television from the council chamber to the press room, so that journalists can write their copy while keeping an eye on the council proceedings.

Part of the proactive strategy being adopted by local authorities results in a wider range of council officers having contact with the media. It is important that these situations are managed by the Public Relations Officer in order to maximize the potential and at the same time reduce the risk of an indiscreet or inappropriate comment being made on controversial issues. Some council employees, even senior managers, may be terrified of speaking to the media. Sometimes perhaps there is the fear of being made to look stupid and partly, too, the dread of saying something incorrect, or 'putting one's foot in it'. The role of the Public Relations Officer in this situation is to ensure that the interviewee knows what is expected of him or her, is fully prepared as to the kind of questions that will be asked and is fully briefed on the answers. Usually it is best if the interviewee is accompanied to the radio or television studio, and, in the case of an interview with a newspaper journalist, it is reassuring for the interviewee to have the Public Relations Officer sitting alongside.

Various private sector consultancies and training specialists now run training courses for staff who are likely to be interviewed by the media. Some of these are very good but it is recommended in all cases that their style and content be evaluated first to ensure that specific needs are met. Some local authorities run media training courses in-house, making use of freelance local broadcasters to lead interview practice sessions. These have the advantage of being tailor-made to the authority's requirements and usually considerably cheaper. As well as the value of the practical sessions to would-be interviewees, use can be made of such courses to explain generally how the media work, how to recognize a 'good story' and even the basics of how to write a media news release. The value of a good picture must never be overlooked in helping to reinforce the impact of a good story in the papers.

Sometimes it is possible to create a so-called photo-opportunity and invite news editors from the local papers to send photographers. In these situations it is vital to give as much notice as possible and to telephone on the day to check whether the photographer will be attending. As far as the opportunity itself is concerned, it is the unusual or action shots that provide the most impact. Generally the press are tired of mayoral line-ups and hand shaking at the presentation of a cheque for charity and a public relations officer can usually damage its reputation if such line-ups are the extent of its creativity.

Nowadays newspapers tend to keep their number of staff photographers to an absolute minimum, and it is often necessary for the public relations

Figure 7.1 *A photograph stands more chance of being used if it is a good action shot. (Reproduced courtesy of Knowsley Metropolitan Borough Council)*

office to organize the production of its own photograph, copies of which will be sent together with the news release to appropriate newspapers. The same rules apply. Pictures must be unusual and it's the action shots that generate the greatest take-up (see Figure 7.1). A professional and accredited photographer should always be used and a range of shots should be taken in order to offer the greatest choice. In some cases it will be necessary to send different shots to different newspapers so that each news editor feels that he or she is getting an exclusive.

It would be misleading, however, to suggest that all the media relations work for a local authority is proactive in style. Inevitably some of the work will be responding to adverse publicity and, in such times of pressure and crisis, a well thought out strategy, and imaginative responses efficiently delivered and based on sound knowledge and judgement can usually save the day. The fact is that in such situations the media require an explanation and the old-fashioned 'No comment' from a nameless spokesperson will satisfy no one. If the media does not have an answer from the council, then it will easily find someone else prepared to offer a view of the situation, and this will sometimes be to the detriment of the local authority.

In some cases it may be possible to turn the situation around to the advantage of the council. For example, in 1992 Knowsley Borough Council heard, ahead of the official publication of figures by the Health Education Authority, that Knowsley was the local authority with the highest number of deaths from smoking-related diseases. Clearly there would be a great deal of media interest at both local and national level. Investigations quickly established that the figures related to data that had been collected three years previously. Since then, in full recognition of the problem, the council had appointed a Health 2000 Coordinator in conjunction with the local health authority and had established support groups for people who wished to give up smoking. Education programmes had been introduced in schools throughout the borough with the aim of highlighting the risks associated with smoking. One school had even written and performed its own anti-smoking play. All the evidence suggested that such a strategy was beginning to show results. So the emphasis changed: the potential bad news became something of a success story, which was reflected in the press coverage subsequently generated.

The impact of media relations

Measuring the success of media relations is notoriously difficult. A simple measure of column centimetres is clearly limited in its usefulness, as is the process favoured by some in the private sector, whereby a value on public relations-generated coverage is set as the cost of an equivalent size of paid-for advertisements. Obviously, though, it is vital to try to put some sort of value or weight against either a specific campaign or on a council's ongoing media relations activity.

Knowsley Borough Council uses a simple ratio of positive to negative news items and features that appear in the press. Admittedly it is not the most scientific method of evaluation; it is open to less than objective interpretation in its measurement, but it does present a result which is easily understandable and which, over a period of time, can indicate trends in coverage and, to a degree, is a useful guide to the performance of a media relations section. In these days when so much of what a local authority does (and how it does it) is subject to performance measurement, it is appropriate for a public relations office to ensure that its performance is kept up to scratch.

Another way in which staff and elected members can be kept up to date with the output and performance of their public relations office is for it to produce a daily and weekly cuttings service. This not only demonstrates where proactive strategies are succeeding, but can also be used to highlight where criticisms of the local authority need to be responded to

Internal communications

Local authorities have had to accept many changes in recent years, and the impact of all of these on employees has been considerable. Legislation has resulted in more work, or, at the very least, in existing work having to be carried out in a different way. The introduction of compulsory competitive tendering requires significant cost-cutting and changes to work practices if the contracts are to remain in-house. The introduction of business units in some authorities, along with the delayering of management structures and reduction in workforces, means that things are now done differently. Employees need to understand why such changes are taking place if they are to continue to make a real contribution to the work of the authority.

A good system and range of internal communications is therefore vital, and increasingly it is becoming the responsibility of the public relations office to ensure that such systems are in place. There are a variety of devices available. Many authorities produce employee newspapers on a regular basis, and these are used to present management messages and information as well as a range of 'newsy' items about employees, past and present. Sometimes in an authority that is spread over a large area it is difficult to ensure a full circulation of these newspapers, and special attention has to be given to those employees who are often away from base or who operate in outlying areas. Presented in a lively and entertaining way, these newspapers can be quite successful in 'spreading the word', although occasionally there is doubt as to whether they are really management mouthpieces or chatty pieces of gossip and news about employees. Almost certainly, in most cases, they are a combination of both.

Some authorities also produce employee bulletins that are clearly a series of messages from the Chief Executive or the Chief Officer Group. These are sometimes supplemented by departmental newsletters. Increasingly, and it is so with all organizations employing large numbers of staff, systems are in place for the briefing of work teams, using the cascading approach to information giving and receiving. This requires well-written briefs being circulated to all team leaders, who in many cases require appropriate training in team-briefing and listening techniques. Some organizations are writting this function into managers' and supervisors' job descriptions, and even making it one of the factors against which performance related pay is calculated.

Knowsley Borough Council regularly holds induction courses for all new employees and also what it calls 'Knowsley Awareness Days' which aim to give employees a greater understanding of the Council's key objectives, together with an appreciation of the progress which is being made in each of these areas. The sessions include informal discussion groups involving a cross-section of staff from all departments and a presentation from the

Chief Executive, who also answers questions and takes part in a discussion with staff.

Visits and visitors

All local authorities play host to a wide range of visitors, and this is an ideal opportunity to present a positive image of the area and the work of the authority. Be it a royal visit or one from a government minister or perhaps from a group representing the borough's twin town, it is essential that the Public Relations Officer is engaged not only in generating some media coverage of the event but also in organizing the detail of the event itself and ensuring that everything goes smoothly and according to plan. In some local authorities this is made easier because the Mayor's Office and asociated civic functions and services are the direct responsibility of the Public Relations Officer.

Knowsley Borough Council holds an annual Open Day when it organizes a range of exhibitions and demonstrations about the work of the council and the services it provides.

Research and evaluation

More and more local authorities are using market research techniques to obtain an understanding of their customers, as well as to receive a closer picture of public attitudes to the council and its services. This serves two purposes. First, it can provide a clear basis for undertaking activities and shaping future policies. Second, it can measure levels of satisfaction with existing services, thereby highlighting areas where new initiatives or changes to existing approaches may be required.

For example one county council commissioned Market and Opinion Research International (MORI) to research the attitudes of residents towards the council and its services. The research was used to develop a communications strategy designed to meet identified needs and communication problem areas.

The MORI report revealed, for example, that 71 per cent of the residents felt that the council did not keep them well-informed. In response, a free newspaper was produced and delivered to every household. The newspaper presented financial information from the annual report in a more readable format. The articles reported on different council services, providing a contact name and telephone number and this initiative now takes place every year.

The MORI report also revealed that libraries topped the list of services (52 per cent), thereby pinpointing an effective means of reaching one in two

news
release

K/106/94   18th July 1994

VIEWS SOUGHT ON KNOWSLEY'S EDUCATION SERVICE

Knowsley is embarking on an ambitious initiative to find out
what parents and pupils think of its Education Service.

In a move which is believed to be the first of its kind in
the country, the Authority has commissioned a series of
research projects including the use of questionnaires, group
discussions and interviews with pupils, parents and teachers
to develop a better understanding of the factors which affect
choice of school.

3750 parents will be asked to complete an in-depth
confidential questionnaire covering factors such as the
availability of suitable and sufficient information on
schools, the plus-points, factors which may put parents off
sending their child to a Knowsley school and indicators which
strongly influence the final choice of school.

The Authority has organised discussion groups with
pupils - those in primary school who are shortly to leave and
11 year olds who have just started secondary school. Views
have been sought on their aspirations and aims for secondary
education and what is most important and whether it lived up
to expectations.

ENDS

Article contains 175 words

FOR FURTHER INFORMATION PLEASE CONTACT:
HEATHER VAUGHAN
TEL 051 443 3536
NIGHT 0831 632289   ed/survey

KNOWSLEY
METROPOLITAN BOROUGH

Figure 7.2 *A Knowsley news release. Note the line spacing and the layout. The design of the news release paper (in Knowsley's corporate colours) is intended to be attractive and eye-catching. Note also the contact name at the bottom of the page, complete with a 24-hour telephone enquiry service. (Reproduced courtesy of Knowsley Metropolitan Borough Council)*

Figure 7.3 *Cuttings from the local papers appearing after the news release about the education survey in Figure 7.2*

residents. A series of free bookmarks was produced, with information about key services and distributed through libraries. As a result of the usefulness of the original survey, follow-up surveys were commissioned in three areas: social services, education and finance. Plans were formulated for regular monitoring of specified services, to measure changes in effectiveness and satisfaction.

Figures 7.2 and 7.3 illustrate a news release by Knowsley Borough Council and the subsequent reactions from the media.

The law and public relations in local government

Public relations officers in local government have an obligation to be aware of their legal responsibilities and to comply with the law, especially in relation to the publication and/or dissemination of material that could be considered overtly political. Local government is empowered, if not required, to communicate its activities through the Local Government Act 1972. Further legislation (Local Government Act 1986) amended the 1972 Act, so that party political publicity by a local authority is expressly prohibited. This Act also included a provision for a statutory Code of Practice on Publicity, which must be taken into account in the commissioning of any public relations activity.

Further, section 27 of the Local Government Act 1988 has strengthened and extended the 1986 Act, placing restrictions on publicity that 'promotes or opposes a point of view on the question of political controversy that is identifiable as the view of one political party and not another'. The implications of Clause 27 are far-reaching, with many believing that the statutory code could result in less communication with the public while also placing severe restrictions on the local government Public Relations Officer. It is to be hoped that commonsense in interpreting and implementing Clause 27 will prevail.

Although these are the primary provisions that cover public relations in local authorities, other powers and requirements to publicize activities are included in legislation relating to specific activities. In addition, the Access to Information Act 1985 makes it a requirement to provide direct access to all council committee reports and to background papers; and from 1994 onwards there is a requirement to publish the Citizen's Charter performance indicators in local newspapers.

8

Public Relations in the Non-commercial Sector

Jane Hammond

The non-commercial sector includes all areas of public life except for commercial companies. Two of these areas – national and local government – are dealt with in the two preceding chapters. This chapter covers the other areas: membership organizations such as professional bodies, trade unions and associations, clubs and societies, housing associations and charities.

When considering the application of public relations to non-commercial organizations, it is essential to remember the way in which they differ from commerce. The ratio of financial to human resources is different. The democratic process in non-commercial organizations means that the Public Relations Officer must often adopt a totally neutral role in a way that does not apply to commerce. Policy-making and executive roles are frequently divorced from one another and internal publics are far more important than in commercial organizations, because of the part members and supporters play in contributing to the success of the organization.

Messages

All organizations must convey messages about themselves, but in many non-commercial organizations messages may be their *raison d'être*. They may have no other purpose beyond communicating what they stand for. This applies to political parties; to campaigning organizations such as Amnesty International, Greenpeace and the Howard League for Penal Reform; to organizations carrying out educational programmes, such as the Women's National Cancer Control Campaign; and to any religious organization (Christian, Jewish, Muslim, Buddhist, etc.).

Even when an organization has an operational role, its effectiveness in conveying its messages may mean the difference between its survival or demise. Trade unions, for instance, must explain to their own members, to the managements with whom they are negotiating and to the public the reasons behind pay claims or industrial action if it occurs. Trade and professional bodies must deliver clear messages about the trades or professions they represent if they are to keep their membership figures healthy. No charity can hope to survive without adequate funding and suitable volunteer support. These are only forthcoming in response to messages spelling out clearly what the charity's objectives and functions are. Sometimes the public have misconceptions about what the charity's work really is, as opposed to what they think it is, as Barnardos found when their research revealed general ignorance about the full range of the charity's work.

If public relations can be defined as encompassing all aspects of an organization's communication, presentation and representation activities, messages are clearly the responsibility of an organization's Public Relations Officer. The importance of ensuring that an organization's messages are received by their target audiences in the way its management wishes cannot be stressed too highly.

Resources

The chief resources of any non-commercial organization are human, as opposed to the commercial sector, where they are mainly financial. Funds can come in a variety of ways, ranging from donations (for charities), subscriptions (for membership organizations) or grants from national or local organizations.

Subscriptions must depend on members' representatives agreeing these at appropriate gatherings or in other suitable ways (so they cannot be adjusted at short notice) and grants are made as a result of deliberations by the decision-makers in the national or local organizations concerned. Such decisions can be heavily influenced by other considerations – political, sectarian, compassionate – over which the recipient organization will have no control.

Charities of course must raise money through activities, such as events, street collections, direct mail, appeals to trusts and other grant-making bodies, or by persuading people to covenant money or leave legacies. None of this can be done effectively without proper public relations support. Fund-raising and public relations are interrelated: donations depend on a charity's image, which in turn depends on the style of the fund-raising. Public relations professionals may find themselves carrying out the fund-raising itself, if the charity is a small one, but generally this is left to professional fund-raisers, as this area of activity has become a very specialized one. Without effective appeals literature, publicity for events and clarification of the message, no fund-raising will be successful.

Charities must be registered by the Charity Commission if they are to derive any benefits from charitable status. The two main benefits that registration gives are that it enables them to recoup tax rebates on covenants and to levy a payroll tax.

Covenants are a popular way of giving money: if donors promise to pay a fixed sum for at least four years, the charity can claim back from the Inland Revenue the money that would have been paid on that sum at the current tax rate. For example, if a donor covenants £100 a year for four years and the rate of tax on that money is 25 per cent, the charity can claim back an additional £25 a year.

A payroll tax is deducted at source by an employer, who then passes on the money to the registered charity.

Whether the organization concerned has ample funds or is struggling with one or two paid staff or none, finance is inevitably an emotive issue. All non-commercial organizations must endeavour to steer clear of accusations of extravagance from any quarter; if proved valid, such accusations may sound the death knell of such organizations, particularly if they are charities.

Nowadays running non-commercial organizations has developed into a separate career with its own qualifications and, at the most senior levels, remuneration that can stand comparison with commercial posts at similar levels. In organizations where such people may be earning more than their paymasters – trade unions for lower-paid workers, for instance – it is particularly important to avoid accusations of extravagance. The lower-paid paymasters are the decision-makers; they decide policy, following recommendations by their officers in precisely the same way as do party politicians in national and local government, following recommendations for their civil servants or local government officers.

The public relations officer has a vital role to play in ensuring that the image projected by the organization is in line with the impression it wishes to give about how it spends its money. This means using channels of communication that are effective without looking extravagant – avoiding the use of expensive paper, for instance, or not running an event that appears to require a surfeit of expensive food and drink merely to indulge those present. Appearances can be deceptive and something that costs a lot of money – say, a publication – will not appear over-expensive if presented in the right way. As with all public relations activities, it is the impression conveyed to target audiences that matters.

Non-commercial organizations usually have to operate within tight financial controls and time scales and are seldom in a position to invest for long-term returns. This applies particularly to charities. Ironically, it is often when an organization is in trouble, financial or otherwise, that it needs to put more resources into public relations but finds it difficult to pay for it.

A non-commercial organization's human resources may, relatively speaking, be of greater importance than those of a commercial organization. All organizations depend for their existence on those who staff them, and consequently on the skill with which such people are selected. Clearly a commercial concern with competent, loyal staff has a much greater chance of success than one poorly managed by incompetent staff with no incentive to be loyal. The same applies to any non-commercial organization, with the difference that, because of the constraints outlined above, staff numbers are likely to be less and their workload greater. This is where unpaid volunteers come into their own.

Volunteers may assist the organization with office work or as collectors of donations, fees or subscriptions at functions or through street collections. As benefactors, donors or sponsors they are tremendously valuable. Above all they serve on the committees and councils that run non-commercial organizations and, in the process, make all the final decisions on policy.

It is essential to remember that volunteer helpers or fund-raisers must be 'paid', just as employers have to be. Volunteers are not paid in the coin of the realm (except sometimes with reimbursement of expenses) but must be substantially rewarded in terms of work satisfaction, expressions of appreciation, enhanced social status and contacts, or in other ways. Sometimes the rewards may come in the form of the emotional satisfaction of sacrificing comfort for the sake of the charity concerned.

Here again the public relations role is vital in understanding these needs and taking them into account when drawing up a programme of activities.

Accountability

Paid staff in non-commercial organizations, while having enormous influence, are accountable to decision-makers who are elected or appointed, either from an organization's own membership or by recruiting appropriate people from outside. This does not apply to small organizations which their members operate by running things themselves in a voluntary capacity. It is precisely when they become large enough to employ paid staff and these volunteers get on the payroll that they can run into trouble!

Chairmen and directors of public companies are accountable to shareholders for their decisions and those of the paid employees responsible to them, but they are given almost total autonomy during the period between shareholders' gatherings, such as annual general meetings, and can take major decisions without constant referral back to shareholders. In the non-commercial sector, on the other hand, all major decisions – and sometimes relatively minor ones – have to be ratified by a committee or council consisting of people elected from the membership or from the ranks of those prepared to volunteer their time.

Sometimes the committee members running an organization may be of a lower social and economic status than those whose executive decisions they are ratifying. Such a situation calls for considerable tact and diplomacy.

Because of the key role played by members, supporters or volunteers in the non-commercial sector, public relations programmes must be extensively discussed and agreed as far down the chain of command as is relevant. Ample time must be allocated to enable objectives to be discussed and agreed as democratically as possible (provided this is in accordance with the organization's philosophy). If this is not done, disaffected individuals can disrupt and sometimes entirely sabotage a programme if they feel insufficient efforts were made to listen to their points of view.

Once a programme is agreed, however, the public relations professionals must make it clear that they expect to carry it out with minimum interference. Having to pay disproportionate attention to committee interference can sap their energy unnecessarily.

This policy of detailed consultation at the start proved very successful with the launch of a fund-raising programme for a South London church, St Matthew's. This enormous Georgian church was trying to raise £5000 in five months for the second phase of a big fund-raising programme to convert the church into a multi-cultural meeting place for Brixton. Fourteen organizations were using the church as a meeting place; they were all represented on the management committee that was seeking to raise the funds. They ranged from the predominantly white, middle-class Brixton Society to a Rastafarian theatre group. They expressed considerable pessimism about the fund-raising programme's chance of success, stressing the deprived nature of the area, but consented to a meeting to discuss the programme's fourteen objectives. After only one change at the meeting, the programme went ahead and the target sum of £5000 was raised in five months, as planned.

Training

Nowadays staff working for non-commercial organizations are expected to be just as professional as those working in commerce; public relations staff are no exception. Because of the financial constraints, there is always too much work for the public relations staff to do properly, yet, as has been shown, the success of any non-commercial organization's activities – indeed sometimes its very survival – is dependent on an extensive programme of public relations work being carried out all the time. The answer is to appoint volunteers to carry out much of the routine work.

The Royal Institution of Chartered Surveyors, for instance, has a network of thirty branches, each with its own press officer, to serve its 90,000 strong membership (70,000 full members and 20,000 in other categories). The press officers liaise with local press in their own areas and are supported in their activities with manuals and headquarters support.

Another organization, which pioneered this approach in 1937, was the National Association of Local Government Officers (NALGO), as it was then known. It is now part of the trade union known as UNISON, formed from a merger between NALGO and two other unions: the Confederation of Health Service Employees (COHSE) and the National Union of Public Employees (NUPE).

UNISON recommends to each of its 1500 or so branches that it appoints a communications officer to handle public relations matters locally. To assist these officers, branches receive a comprehensive pack describing the functions of a public relations officer, explaining how to produce branch publications and giving guidance on media relations, with instructions on news release writing and on print production, campaigning, recruitment, proof-correcting and legal matters. The guidance notes are of a high enough standard to be of use to anyone starting public relations work in any organization, yet easy enough to be understood by people of varying levels of education.

Each of the union's thirteen regions has a network of lay members, who can give support when needed. For instance, they assist with training courses, contribute to the success of campaigns in their own regions and in some cases help with the production of regional bulletins. The full-time headquarters public relations staff support the work of their volunteer colleagues by running regular training courses for them and visiting and being in contact with them regularly.

The roles of UNISON's volunteer public relations officers are very clearly defined, so that they do not stray into areas best left to the professionals, but their work is invaluable at local and regional level. Whenever anything is in the news concerning UNISON members – a pay claim, a dispute or a settlement – the regional district and branch activists will be in contact with local journalists, with whom they are expected to develop good relationships, so that the union's point of view can be put clearly and in relation to local issues.

Professional public relations staff will also find themselves training members if they work for trade associations. In these instances the members may be small companies not able to afford professional public relations advice from consultants, but anxious to use public relations techniques in developing their businesses. To meet these needs, many trade associations run seminars, include professional advice in their newsletters and maintain close contact on such matters with members. A West Country trade association of food producers, for instance, runs a day's seminar to help winners of annual food awards to make the most of their awards through publicity.

Politics

Non-commercial public relations has been described as 'public relations in a political climate'. This is because, whether the public relations is practised in an overtly political setting-such as a political party, a local authority or a government department or organization – or for a membership or other voluntary organization or charity, internal politics are always very significant, and must be taken into account. This will be evident from the prominence given to the part played by committee members in the running of a non-commercial organization.

There is one way in which party politics are especially relevant to charities: they must steer clear of them. The Charity Commission stipulates that, to achieve charitable status, an organization must either relieve poverty, advance religion, advance education or benefit the community. It must not, on the other hand, seek to change or retain a law or seek a particular line of administration.

In the past this has inhibited many charities from speaking out about situations which they see as impeding their work, although the Charity Commissioners are now becoming more flexible. In 1988, for instance, the South African Embassy complained to the Charity Commissioners about Christian Aid's request to its supporters to complain to the Embassy about the effect of the war in Mozambique on Christian Aid's projects in that country. The Commissioners replied that they had no objection to a charity seeking to alert its supporters, as well as the general public, to the difficulties placed in the way of the charity fulfilling its charitable objects, and found no deliberate intention of engaging in a political campaign. In the past other charities who had made similar points ran the risk of losing their charitable status.

The situation is different now. In a pamphlet published in March 1994 the Charity Commission states that charities must still refrain from seeking 'to influence public opinion or put pressure on the government...to legislate or adopt a particular policy...' They must also refrain from participating in party political demonstrations, conducting referenda or engaging in any other overt political activities.

On the other hand, charities may now actively engage in seeking to 'influence government or public opinion through well-founded, reasonable argument based on research or direct experience on issues either relating directly to the achievement of the charity's own stated purposes or relevant to the well-being of the charitable sector'. In mid-1994, for instance, Christian Aid launched a campaign seeking to influence the policies of the World Bank and the IMF, because the charity believed current policies were having an adverse rather than beneficial effect on the condition of the poorest of the world's population. Christian Aid's campaign, incidentally, is an excellent example of good public relations in practice – only to be expected from a charity whose former public relations officer was for many years a very active member of the Institute of Public Relations.

Strategy

Since public relations work is a professional activity that can be practised by or for any organization, all principles of public relations hold good wherever it is practised, and non-commercial organizations are no exception. As in any other field, it is essential to research and analyse what the particular situation is, what the objectives should be and who the target audiences are. Apart from the usual strategic reasons, such fine-tuning helps the organization to conserve its resources by preventing it from wasting money on areas that are not important to the programme under consideration.

When identifying its audiences, any non-commercial organization should place particular emphasis on internal audiences – including volunteers, supporters and committee members, as relevant – as well as employees, because of the important part such people play in the organization.

Although there will never be any over-abundance of finance for communication channels such as print, video, film and other mechanical methods, non-commercial organizations can find other channels of communication more open to them than to commercial organizations. Methods particularly relevant to non-commercial organizations follow.

Media relations

Media relations are particularly useful to the non-commercial organization, as all three of the communication media – press, television and radio – are often much more willing to give editorial coverage to its activities than to those of commercial organizations. This is because commercial organizations are often seeking coverage for activities that the media perceive as promotional, with a vested interest. Communication media that depend on advertising for their survival consider that promotional publicity should, in many cases, be given through advertising, and that commercial companies are seeking 'free' advertising space. Much of the news non-commercial organizations are disseminating is of considerable interest. This is almost always the case where charities are concerned. A publication or radio station will often be predisposed to publicize a charitable event, even if a commercial company is also likely to benefit.

A first novel, for instance, can often attract publicity if the author announces that some of the royalties will go to a charity that bears some relation to the book's subject matter. A fashion show is more likely to get advance publicity if some of the proceeds go towards a charity that has some connection with the show.

Trade associations, trade unions and professional bodies can often attract editorial coverage because they represent interests across an industry or profession rather than the narrow commercial interest of one firm. The annual European Fishing Tackle Trade Exhibition, for instance, attracts considerable editorial coverage because it is organized by the European Fishing Tackle Trade Association, a mainly European-wide body with no vested interest in any particular company or country. This would not attract nearly so much publicity if the exhibition was mounted by a commercial interest such as a trade publication.

Most of the non-commercial organizations also attract pictorial publicity, again because of the human interest angle. Events can attract an extensive amount of coverage.

It is important that relevant personnel in non-commercial organizations have adequate training in responding to the media. It is also essential that everyone realizes the importance of not treating contacts with journalists lightly, for nothing is ever really 'off-the-record'.

House publications

House publications – internal and external, newsletters, bulletins, magazines, newspapers – are essential to the survival of non-commercial organizations. A regular internal publication, for instance, can serve as a publicity medium to project the organization to outside target groups as well as performing its internal role. Sending local newspapers or radio stations newsletters from a small group, such as a branch of a big organization or a pressure group, can keep those media in touch with what is happening. The journalists who receive the publications regularly become familiar with the organization concerned.

Apart from keeping members, supporters and target groups up to date with what is happening and keeping morale high by maintaining interest and enthusiasm, house publications can play a valuable part in defining the personalities of the organizations they serve. Many non-commercial organizations, because they may be concerned with disseminating information or conveying messages or representing groups of people, can often lack definition as far as their internal and external publics are concerned. House publications can rectify this situation.

The publication can, for instance, publish profiles of the key people in the organization, include photographs of people and events and run correspondence columns where people can air their views. Public relations staff who edit such publications must equip themselves with some journalistic train-ing in order to do the job properly, and should take steps to ensure that they get a steady flow of contributions. This can be done by persistently asking everyone, whenever the occasion arises, if there is anything to go into the next issue. Correspondence can be stimulated by encouraging anyone who has a point of view to give it verbally. If it is taken down and sent to the person concerned with a suggestion that the text is published over the person's name and the person authorizes this, a satisfactory exchange of correspondence can begin to develop in a relatively painless way.

Internal communication

A cornerstone of any internal communication programme is the programme of regular publications of the type mentioned above. An active internal communication programme is so essential to any non-commercial organization that without it such an organization will wither and die. If the organization is a charity, supporters must know what is happening to their donations and how the committee members are running the organi-zation. If the organization is a membership one, members must feel their subscriptions are being put to good use; subscriptions must continue to come in as the future of the organization depends on them. If the organi-zation is a pressure group or a trade union running a campaign on its members' behalf, there must be a consistent approach in presenting the message.

Internal communications enable the internal publics to play their part in achieving success for the organization. As already mentioned, members in membership organizations can perform important public relations roles, so they must receive and consequently deliver consistent messages. If the organization is one promoting a cause, such as a pressure group or political or religious organization, the public relations programme will run into obvious difficulties if the cause is presented in conflicting ways rather than in one consistent way.

Events

Events are important to all non-commercial organizations. They have fund-raising potential for charities, they have recruitment potential for any organization needing members and supporters, they can bring together everyone concerned with an issue and provide feedback from members and other target audiences. They can attract media coverage, confer prestige on the organization and boost morale generally. They can also provide excel-lent photo-opportunities.

Social events can, like publications, assist in defining the personality of any organization, depending on the style of an event and the part played by members, supporters and staff. They also provide an invaluable means of saying 'thank you' for the efforts made, often considerable and almost always unpaid, by those supporting the organization in different ways.

The importance of events to charities can be out of all proportion to the sums raised. If the event is fairly small or may cost a lot to put on, the returns from the event in cash terms may seem negligible. In those circumstances organizers may feel they might just as well have written out a cheque for the amount raised and saved themselves the bother. The value of such events, however, lies in the publicity they attract, especially if it is quite obvious that considerable effort is being made at the 'grass roots' and if there is a good news angle. In one fund-raising exercise for a community centre, for instance, Marks & Spencer was so impressed with the commitment shown by groups in what was a deprived area that it willingly agreed to finance a lift for the building. The major donors, such as trusts, foundations and other grant-giving bodies, take such commitment into account when deciding on whether or not to give funds to projects.

When talking about fund-raising methods for charities, it is tempting to paraphrase Sir Christopher Wren when asked by a gushing woman where she could see examples of his work; he told her, 'Madam, look around you'. Any member of the public is frequently at the receiving end of fund-raising activities: direct mail; street collections; appeals to attend a concert, play, dance or disco, or join in a sponsored walk or swim; litter collection or whatever – the list is almost endless. To be successful, all fund-raising activities must be properly planned with effective public relations support. They should have realistic targets, but not too low; it is surprising how much money people can raise if there is sufficient motivation and expertise.

Sponsorship

Sponsorship provides valuable opportunities for partnership with commercial interests to the mutual benefit of both parties. By underwriting projects, sponsors can enable organizations to undertake ventures that might otherwise be too risky. It can provide a valuable way of extending a programme of activities in a cost-effective way. Sponsorship money, however, is wasted without adequate public relations support – in other words, if the sponsor provides support for a project and the organization makes no effort to publicize this support, the sponsor will not be anxious to repeat the exercise.

Exhibitions

Exhibition organizers often offer non-commercial organizations free space at exhibitions. For instance, the National Nursing and Care Homes Exhibition, which features nursing home equipment, offers free stand space to professional organizations concerned with the care of people in nursing homes. Along with that goes an entry in the exhibition catalogue – all good publicity for the organization. Such opportunities are sometimes wasted because the staff of such organizations underestimate the degree to which such opportunities can help their public relations programmes.

Even if the stand space is not free but the exhibition is relevant, the organization should still give very serious consideration to taking part and, having made the decision, should ensure that the opportunity is used well. There is nothing more damaging to an organization's reputation than a badly staffed and managed exhibition stand. But with enthusiastic participation by members and skilful direction by the public relations staff, taking stand space at an exhibition can be of great benefit.

As with other activities, some training should be given to those taking part to ensure they assist in presenting the organization and its activities in the right way.

Opinion leaders and formers

Every charity makes use of opinion leaders and formers to attract support for its activities, as can be seen from the famous names that adorn the letterheads of almost any charity. Such people give essential third-party endorsement to an organization and, if they are celebrities, confer valuable prestige.

Opinion leaders stimulate fund-raising, recruitment and attendance at events, and in many other ways benefit the organization. Journalists come into the category of opinion formers, since their comments will play an important part in influencing public reactions to any organization.

Advertising

Financial constraints mean that advertising is not employed widely. Some of the charities, however, use advertising extensively in their fund-raising campaigns. In such cases the advertising is handled through advertising agencies in the usual way.

Advertising must not be ruled out for smaller organizations, however, as such organizations, especially charities, are sometimes given free space in publications in which they can place their own advertisements. If this opportunity occurs, the public relations officer must turn advertising agent and create effective advertising copy, since it is not usually worthwhile using an agency for such small-scale efforts.

Commercial enterprises

A recent development has been the growth of charity shops and catalogues through which charities can raise money by selling goods – either their own or, in some of the shops, goods that are given to them. (They have of course always been able to raise money through jumble sales.)

Every Christmas, members of the public can select well-designed and well-made goods from catalogues sent out by charities through direct mail or enclosed with newspapers and magazines. Christmas cards can be ordered from such catalogues and also bought in some high-street shops.

Evaluation

A proper evaluation exercise must be carried out on every public relations programme, and this can only be done effectively when the situation is adequately researched and analysed and the objectives are properly defined. Evaluation has always been important for the non-commercial sector, since those engaged in it – members, supporters, volunteers or staff – must feel reassured that the organization is giving value for money.

Where finance is limited, extensive professional research programmes are out of the question, but other indicators, such as media coverage, attendance at functions, changes in membership recruitment or its rise or fall, levels of enquiries and success in fund-raising, can all tell their own story. Public relations staff and others, as appropriate, should be particularly careful to keep members and supporters informed through reporting on media coverage, circulating press cuttings and reporting generally on results.

Much informal qualitative and quantitative research can of course take place by circulating questionnaires to members, holding discussion groups, taking straw polls at meetings and generally keeping a close check on results.

Summary

In general, public relations practice in the non-profit-making field must always bear in mind the constraints described in this chapter. Opportunities for creative programmes abound, however, and should be pursued energetically.

9

Parliamentary relations and lobbying

Douglas Smith

The skills required for effective government relations vary little from those of successful military commanders over the centuries. Close and realistic appraisal of the current scene; intelligent preparation for the attack, including the enlistment of allies; effective communication; correct timing; identification of targets; and persistent pressure (courage, if you like) in pressing the attack home.

A bellicose, and some may therefore feel an inappropriate, analogy. Certainly, as indeed in many wars, actual conflict can often be avoided by properly long-sighted policy and appropriate action at early stages. But the similarities remain considerable. Reconnaissance, resolution and effective individual as well as group performance lie at the heart of most lobbying victories, as they do in the bloodiest of battles.

The very word 'lobbying' also has for many an unpleasant ring to it: an improper and somewhat sleazy manipulation of the pure political processes. That is unfortunate and largely incorrect, just as were the sneering references so often heard to the words 'public relations' in the early years of its growth. Lobbying in political circles dates back for centuries, and, while not the oldest profession nor necessarily sanctified by age, remains an entirely correct way to proceed if ground rules are followed.

There is, however, a small group of government affairs practitioners who see their activities as having little or nothing to do with 'public relations' as such. It could be argued that they are in error. The majority of campaigns and most ongoing government relations activity calls not only for a clear analysis of problems and opportunities (as we have said) but also effective communication of messages to newspapers, radio and television as well as political audiences. Media pressure is a key factor in the success, or failure, of most causes. And if proper handling of the media is not part of public relations, one would be interested to know what is.

That being said, there are specialist features of this branch of our profession that are essential to success and can cause major calamity to those who blunder in without awareness of them. It is of course equally true for other areas of public relations (financial, pharmaceutical, high tech) and for broadly the same reasons. One needs to know how the system works in order to begin influencing it. *How* do policies evolve? *What* makes civil servants and politicians tick? *Why* should action be taken at a certain stage? *Who* precisely should be targeted? *Where* should they be met and when? As you can see Kipling's six faithful serving men – Who, Why, What, When, Where and How – apply here as much as anywhere in public relations, marketing or advertising. Let us therefore settle for government relations being seen as part of effective corporate communications but in a particularly important area, since the effect of political action is so far-ranging, with a dramatic impact on all of us.

Legislation lies at the heart of any government affairs programme. Initiating laws, amending them, or attempting even to stop them entirely, is what this business is about. Crudely phrased, you may well think, for such a majestic area of activity. But then the whole process of lawmaking in Britain, and indeed more widely, is not as pristine an exercise as the constitutional history books would have one believe.

In theory the British procedure is well-known. Parties are democratically elected on a policy platform. They then introduce laws to put these principles into effect. The legislation is carefully researched, with all interested groups consulted, and then equally carefully framed by experienced legal draughtsmen. MPs and peers debate principle and examine detail in committees; and at the end Her Majesty the Queen puts her name to an Act of Parliament.

Not always so in reality. To look back only a few years, one can find examples of Bills rushed through under a wave of media-aroused pressure – the Dangerous Dogs Act, for example. As a result of excessive speed, there were flaws in the wording of this Act that are (as I write) still being disputed in the courts.

Then we have the infamous Poll Tax exercise. Principally under pressure from a determined Prime Minister, a Community Charge was introduced to replace Britain's former rating system, which, however illogical in places, at least had the value of being simple and workable. The new tax was not – as many, including Conservative MPs, had warned would be the case. Yet the Whips cracked and the system duly changed, only to be reversed a few years later. Billions of pounds of public money and millions of hours of administrative time were wasted as a result.

These examples are given not to castigate any one government or ridicule those ministers particularly concerned but simply to stress how logic and commonsense do not always apply in politics. It therefore pays never to be complacent and assume that it will.

A wise government affairs programme spends much time studying the origins of legislation, because the best time to amend or prevent is at the very start of the process. Monitor activity in the so-called (and occasionally correctly) political 'Think Tanks'. During the long Margaret Thatcher regime, thoughts emerging from, say, the Institute of Economic Affairs or the Adam Smith Institute were frequently a force in initiating Bills. Under any Labour Government it will be the same, but of course from a different origin. It pays to have regard for these groups as well; in a democracy, governments change. And then there is, increasingly and powerfully, the European Union – its Commission in Brussels and Parliament in Strasbourg. Proposals emerging from both areas need the closest attention, and to be fair, inspection and informed comment are often welcomed by them.

A cautionary tale on the need for advance intelligence is provided by one of the world's largest toy manufacturers, the American-owned Hasbro company. Some years back the firm was astonished to learn that all its products were liable to be banned from entering France just ahead of the peak Christmas sales period. The threat was a little-known European Community regulation that allowed such action against extra-EC products when they could be said to endanger an ailing EC national industry. Application had been made to Brussels by French toymakers on those grounds. The decision to act or not would be taken solely by Commission officials, who of course administer as well as propose regulations within the European Union.

There was little time and less lobbying machinery to argue against the proposal, which duly came to pass. Subsequently larger toy manufacturers have formed a European-wide trade association and generally set proper monitoring systems in place. But the absence of them cost Hasbro millions of pounds within two months.

If our emphasis so far has been on defensive action, we should never forget there can be major advantages in actually initiating the process of change. Too many groups – companies and institutions especially – tend to react rather than proact. Yet often they can benefit from a positive stance. Everyone at Westminster recalls the multinational that encouraged legal introduction of reflective number plates for road vehicles when it was at the time the only large manufacturer of the product. Financial rewards were considerable and richly deserved as a result of an initiative for the public good as well as its own.

The basis of a plan of action for all government affairs activity is now emerging, one trusts, from this lengthy preamble. In essence there are three basic stages:

1 *Reconnaissance* – the need for wide background intelligence far ahead of the current political scene, but also a keen eye kept on more immediate events.
2 *Communications* – conveying one's message in an appropriate form to the right audience at the right moment. This presupposes sensible analysis of the issue in question, including identification of targets, enemies and allies.
3 *Pressure* – the need to argue the case, take advantage of every opportunity arising, motivate allies, and demonstrate a proper determination to succeed. But never exclude sensible 'settlements'. As Disraeli said, 'Compromise is the language of politics'.

Reconnaissance

All successful political programmes begin with research. This is entirely right, provided they do not become obsessed with it. 'Paralysis by analysis' is a not uncommon failing. Yet there remains no substitute not only for the strategic view already described but also for practical assessment of who actually matters in deciding things.

Key civil servants must, for example, be identified. Rarely are they the people at the very top. Someone at a lower level is likely to advise and perhaps even assist far more effectively. This is equally true with the politicians. No point in troubling a cabinet minister with matters under the control of a junior – indeed that junior could well be offended by such an approach. Which backbench MPs and peers have an interest in the issue? If there is a constituency concern, e.g. a factory within his or her seat, then the MP is likely to be supportive to any reasonable cause. Some MPs, in addition, are known for their specialist interests; discover who they are by looking through past Parliamentary Questions and the many All-Party Groups active in Parliament each year. And do not exclude their Lordships – usually wise old birds whose contribution to the detail of government is considerable.

Having researched the issues, identified allies (as well as potential enemies it does not pay to stir up), and become clear on the decision-making target, you must then pay careful consideration to timing. Many campaigns fail because they are launched too early or, more frequently, far too late.

An example of success stemming from quick assessment of issues, targets and timely movement can be found in the Foxley Wood story. It is worthy of a brief case history here.

In the late 1980s the then Secretary of State for the Environment threw part of Hampshire into anger and alarm by suddenly saying he was 'minded' (splendid ministerial expression) to allow the building of some 5000 houses at Foxley Wood. Such a move would have gone against the recommendations of one of his own inspectors following a full public inquiry. Residents still felt the site was unsuitable and the decision should be fought.

Problems facing those brought in at short notice by the local council to assist were considerable. There was an acknowledged need for new housing in Hampshire but nobody wanted to have the site in their area – the familiar NIMBY (Not in My Back Yard) factor. Accordingly, while openly sympathetic, other areas in Hampshire were quietly relieved the proposals affected someone other than themselves. Only immediate residents and therefore a few politicians were aroused. Another difficulty lay in the timing. The troublesome decision had been made in late July as Parliament was departing for the summer holidays. No action could be openly taken at Westminster for three months, by which time it could be too late.

There were, however, opportunities for the objectors. The overturning of an inspector's recommendation could be seen as basically alarming. It might be a precedent for other such moves, throwing the whole planning system into disarray. More important, the Secretary of State in question was moving office and his successor was known to be sympathetic on environmental issues. A key objective was therefore quickly to persuade him not to be bound by his predecessor's view.

Strategy fell into three main sections:

1 To maintain loud local opposition but also extend this into national media by stressing how a fundamental principle was being violated. Through energetic use of every news opportunity and well planned protest events, Foxley Wood quickly became a well-known issue.
2 To concentrate pressure on the new Secretary of State. His first major speech was scheduled for the Conservative Party Conference at Blackpool in October. Accordingly a meeting was fixed for the previous evening, and all Tory councillors attending the Conference were invited. Protest posters and badges were prepared.
3 To propose another and environmentally more acceptable site for new house-building in Hampshire: in short, providing the Government with a better alternative rather than simply calling for rejection of Foxley Wood.

Pressure mounted over the August/September period, but ahead of the Blackpool Conference the most shrewd move of the campaign was taken. A private meeting was arranged with the Secretary of State. He was told exactly what was being planned at the Conference and the media activity proposed to cover protests then to be made. Details of the alternative site were left with him for closer study.

Faced with a serious party dispute on his debut and now aware of another choice of site, Mr Secretary sensibly reversed his predecessor's decision. Loud and long were plaudits to him at the Conference where, in his speech, he said how he had taken account of local and national feelings.

Thus the campaign was a success over, in effect, two months, as a result of clear identification of targets and timing, not to mention some very hard background and media work. Foxley Wood remains to this day in its original bosky state.

A final word on the need for good intelligence. Campaigns are invariably far longer than the case history we have given and so can often benefit from the ongoing cut and thrust of political life. Accordingly, it pays to monitor parliamentary activity on a daily basis to seize opportunities by, for example, giving evidence to select committee reports or contributing to debates through friendly members or lords.

This is far too complex an area to expand upon in detail and the need for specialist help is obvious. There are companies that monitor parliamentary and European Union activity efficiently, and at relatively low cost. Unless you have your own specialist researcher or a taste for reading vast quantities of paper, you are well-advised to make use of them. Indeed, since European activity is increasingly vital, support from a Brussels-based research office is also now essential. Without it the Eurocrats will be upon you without warning.

Communications

The value of a carefully constructed message is shown by the Foxley Wood case history. It is of course important in whatever field of public relations one practises but in government relations there are subtle and important differences to note.

Whereas a press release for some commercial product will rarely include mention of any competition and their wares, such simplicity is not advisable in the political arena. Everyone knows that issues always have two or more sides to them. You may properly propose that one point of view is more important than another, and your political allies may well agree, but they will still wish to be informed of counter opinions if only to be ready to oppose them.

Few friends are won, or campaigns either, when a black and white presentation of one's case is thrust into the scene. The issue must be carefully explained and all the arguments rehearsed if sensible support is to be won from others. Yet such are the pressures on politicians' and civil servants' time that no long dissertations will be readily absorbed. Hence the need for pithy writing skills backed by powerful research papers.

An appreciation that you do not approach a left-wing politician in quite the same language and manner as one from the right also helps. As does realization that no two politicians from whatever party are exactly alike. Know your person, his/her background and ambitions, before pen is put to paper or meetings arranged.

Equally, the manner of meetings is important. Anything lengthy must be avoided. Full-blown lunches are, contrary to tradition, not the most welcome first approach – although there are famous exceptions. A terse and well informed fifteen minutes' chat, backed by the right papers and a clear indication of action, is usually more acceptable, especially if those you speak to can see some publicity or constituency advantage to it all. It would be quite wrong for me to suggest that politicians can be consumed with self-interest, just as civil servants are not all over-cautious and pedantic. Yet they live in a world where re-election is essential, and success often flows not simply by being good but also by seeing others are told about it. That is a role the public relations practitioner can well play and, if it helps the general cause, indeed why not?

Only the foolish ignore talking to peers at least as much as to MPs. For a number of reasons, but principally because it is often only a small change one is seeking to make to legislation, one stands a better chance of success in the Upper House.

The Commons has, after all, more of a party political battleground, as anyone who watches its affairs sees. Party discipline is accordingly stronger, and those who wish to amend legislation find it hard to achieve a majority either in committee or on the floor of the house, regardless of the sense of their case. There are exceptions to this rule – mainly when a substantial revolt has been stirred on the Government's backbenches through constituency pressure – but withdrawals on even small points are rare once a Bill has been introduced, further strengthening our argument that the time to act is earlier at drafting and civil service levels.

The Upper House nonetheless offers real opportunities for amendment. There is by no means the same built-in government majority. Regular attenders include many of the 200 or so crossbench or independent peers. Most of these, and others with firmer party tags, are expert at something, and, equally important, prepared to look at a case on its merits rather than the political proclivities.

Their lord and ladyships do not of course have as strong a constituency base as elected members. A direct approach is therefore necessary. Nor are the majority able to call on secretarial support, so it pays to have any proposed amendments ready to hand. But do not for a moment believe you will be dealing with anything other than the most acute minds, who need convincing before they agree to act. Those who have taken this time and trouble have been well rewarded for their efforts. There have been many more reversals of government policy in the Upper than the Lower House over recent years.

These basic lessons in communication – tailor-making the case for the listener and letting them have their say – apply equally to lobbying at other levels. Members of the European Parliament do not, except in Britain, have constituencies as such, and therefore lobbying must take account of their other interests. These are usually party political. Careful identification of personal background and the key players in each group or committee is crucial. Only rarely is this a British MEP; one could well be dealing with a respected Spanish socialist or a German 'green'.

By contrast, if one's target lies in local government, then the constituency springboard is crucial. Obviously decisions are taken here on party lines but many are approached on a wider basis. Even then the reaction of their immediate neighbourhood supporters will bear heavily upon councillors of every persuasion. So any message needs to be locally framed and founded on good officer advice. Never is it more important in lobbying to identify key officers than when approaching the town or county hall. Fortunately most are open and helpful to any proper request for facts.

Pressure

Let us assume battle has now been joined and the case we are currently arguing lies before ministers, MPs and others to do with the process. The watchwords now are vigilance, vigour and verve.

Vigilance is required because one must watch every move by opponents as well as look for every chance to seize opportunities. There are many examples where modest parliamentary occasions – a Ten Minute Rule Bill, or an Adjournment Debate – have been used to maintain momentum for a campaign. They are not, as we say, major events in themselves, but can act as a peg upon which news stories can be given to journalists who specialize in the political scene.

Here indeed is an advantage for the government affairs specialist that other public relations colleagues will envy. There is a large and active group of media in Westminster (and, to an extent in Brussels also) only too keen to latch on to the worthwhile story and run with it. Remember, lobby correspondents can harry ministers face to face when they are in parliamentary places without civil servants to protect them. Such impact can be important. It keeps up pressure and of course may win more advocates to the cause. But, often equally important, it stimulates one's supporters. MPs who appear on television or in the national press fighting the cause are hardly likely to be unhappy about the publicity they have gained and remain enthusiastic to see more of it. Equally clients see progress – again no bad thing.

Vigour is therefore also essential. It is not always easy to maintain. Parliamentary procedures can be long and often tedious. Loyalties are frequently fickle. Yet persistence, the fourth necessary quality, can bring its rewards, as the 1989 Dock Work Bill proved.

In 1987 there was discontent among a number of newly elected Conservative MPs especially against their own Government's refusal to set up the Dock Labour scheme. The ministerial view was that the scheme was dying on its own accord and it was not worth risking a strike to remove it.

Campaigning to change this policy, the MPs used techniques too often derided by more academic lobbyists. There was an Early Day Motion signed by more than 200 MPs, speeches in remote debates, a Ten Minute Rule Bill, fringe meetings at the Conservative Party Conference of 1988, a booklet from the Centre for Policy Studies, another successful Early Day Motion, and parliamentary questions just ahead of the 1989 Budget. All these moves built and sustained public interest. Eventually the Government gave in and a White Paper duly led to the Dock Work Bill, which became law in July 1989.

This determined band of Conservative MPs enjoyed a great advantage – direct access to government. A request from a few backbenchers to meet privately with the minister concerned is not likely to be refused. It can even be manoeuvred in the House itself, where the protective screen of civil servants is happily absent. But that line of approach remains open to any well-organized lobby that has the ability to convince a group of MPs of the rightness of its cause. It is indeed often the greatest advantage MPs can bring to any campaign.

As a point of pressure the Upper House also has advantages one should not neglect. Their Lordships Question Time allows for mini-debates during which the ministers concerned can be probed in a way often disconcerting to them if the arguments are strong. One is not suggesting the world at large watches such encounters with bated breath, but within the framework of government important messages can thereby be communicated.

To summarize, the three broad processes we have outlined here – reconnaissance, communications, pressure – are clearly crudely drawn and overlap in many stages of any programme. Yet they apply broadly to all government relations activity, whether it relates to the UK Parliament, the local town or county hall or the wider European Community within which, increasingly, we live and work.

European Community

A broad conclusion must therefore cover the European Community – a phrase deliberately chosen to embrace not simply those within the present European Union but others who have membership of a wider Council of

Europe. The United Kingdom is of course currently closely involved in the Union but we should still not neglect its Council ties, the more so since they are likely to be increasingly important as business and contacts extend eastwards into newly emerging democracies.

This is no place to attempt any in-depth description of the European Union's constitutional framework or even that of its less fashionable elder sister, the Council of Europe. It is a fast evolving as well as complex picture. As a result, however, effective monitoring is even more essential. On average at least 7000 pieces of either draft or final legislation emerge in the European Union alone each year. Their status varies widely and specialist skill is required to establish priorities.

Broadly speaking, proposals for legislation in the European Union start as a Commission 'situation paper', which is then used as a basis for consultation. Groups organized on a Union-wide rather than national basis are favoured, which is why life has recently been breathed into so many previously dormant international trade associations. A draft proposal is then sent to both Council of Ministers and the European Parliament, the latter studying it by specialist standing committee. This will duly report back for a full vote in the Parliament on any amendments as well as the original proposal.

The Council of Ministers will have been discussing the same proposal in working groups and COREPER (senior permanent national representatives in Brussels), of which Britain has a part. That is called UKREP, staffed by some sixty officials drawn from Whitehall departments.

The Commission tries to reconcile any differing views to reach what is grandly known as a 'Common Position'. The law then appears in the official journal when, if a directive, it must be enacted by all the member states. Recommendations, regulations and decisions (the three other EU lawmaking processes) vary in their strength and purpose.

This outline of the process has been given principally to demonstrate how the European tendency is towards compromise following consultation – in sharp contrast to British Parliamentary habits, where confrontation is far more in evidence. This allows scope for sophisticated lobbying but equally calls for greater resources to be available. One's ideal 'lobby' is able to act in, currently, twelve national centres as well as in Brussels and Strasbourg. An expensive furrow to plough but then the stakes can be high!

The battle for duty free

Delving briefly into history, the campaign run in 1982 by the British Airports Authority (BAA) to protect its income from the duty-free airport shops has several features to demonstrate how lobbying can be effective in the European Union.

The problem arose as a result of trading from so-called 'Butterboats' – ships that sold tax free dairy goods on day trips just outside territorial waters in the Baltic. In July 1981 the European Court ruled their sales illegal, a decision raising fears that the Commission would now act more widely on the duty-free issue. It was, after all, arguable that the principle of duty-free sales for people travelling within the Community is illogical in a common market.

Action took two forms. The first was to highlight the risk to duty-free shops, which, some surveys revealed, were used by a far wider social group than many had believed. The second was to push for legislation to clear up uncertainty in this whole area, thus guarding against future Commission action.

Media activity was considerable and compelling. Loss of income to governments and, more important ahead of European Parliament elections, loss of popularity as well were both featured. By early 1983 the Commission duly compromised its stance.

Once again the familiar lessons emerge, i.e. knowing exactly when, where and how to bring pressure.

Conclusion

A final point applies to government affairs activity just as strongly as to public relations in a wider sense. It is, quite simply, the need for a low profile stance by the lobbyists themselves.

Often one can be tempted to put clients' cases for them when, in reality, politicians always prefer to hear it from the horse's mouth. It is the same with publicity. Let others bask in the limelight, not the lobbyist. As the bard said: 'Nothing so becomes a man as modest stillness and humility'. An entirely appropriate note on which to conclude.

10

Consultancy public relations

Neville Wade

In a sense all public relations practitioners are 'consultants', just as those whom they advise are 'clients', regardless of whether an individual works in an in-house public relations department or for a consultancy firm. In both cases the approach taken to the delivery of professional services is similar. An issue or situation is analysed, the desired outcome interpreted as quantifiable objectives, the critical audiences to whom messages will be addressed identified, the messages themselves translated as a communication strategy, an action plan developed and implemented, and results monitored and evaluated against objectives. However, the significant difference between in-house and consultancy practice is that in the former the practitioner is working for a single organization whilst, in the latter, attention is divided among a number of clients.

One of the many continuing debates among public relations people is centred on the relative merits of in-house versus consultancy public relations services. In most cases this is a sterile discussion, since both 'sides' of the argument are generally complementary and serve a particular purpose. Naturally this is not a rule and there are many exceptions. For example, there are still some large corporate organizations that maintain substantial public relations departments and consider that the service of an external consultant is never appropriate. Equally, there are examples of companies that, over recent years, have reduced the number of in-house personnel to a small core. To support this team on an operational basis, and also to provide special services when needed, outside consultants are called in as required. The important conclusion to draw from this is that there are no hard and fast rules about the nature of consultancies, nor how they should be used. The situation is entirely fluid and develops in fresh directions to meet changing needs. In very much the same way the nature and style of consultancies has altered as the practice of public relations has become more specialized and as the value of that specialist advice and support is more readily recognized.

In looking at the nature of consultancies it is useful, first, to consider how the different forms might be categorized. There are two broad groups: those that have a vertical specialization and those that are more horizontally oriented:

1   *Vertical* consultancies are those firms that have chosen to specialize either in a field of practice or in a type of client. For example, there are consumer consultancies, which concentrate on those clients whose aim is to reach the mass market; there are public affairs specialists, which deal with issues and the matters influencing legislation; there are business-to-business consultancies, which concentrate on another marketing area; and there are specialists in high technology, the environment, employee relations, local authority communication needs and many other fields.

2   *Horizontally* structured consultancies are those offering a range of services, often through a number of internal divisions or departments. Such firms may well embrace both consumer and business-to-business communications and offer those same clients corporate services such as public affairs and employee communication. Indeed there is an increasing trend for such consultancies to stretch the range of their services beyond what has hitherto been regarded as the 'below-the-line' limit of public relations practice. This is in recognition of the fact that public relations is not a finite science and has to develop and change to reflect and react to the world in which practitioners operate. Some consultancies prefer to adopt descriptive styles, which are more akin to management consultancy, and which recognize that the communication function has an impact on every facet of an organization.

The concept of integrated communication, also known as one-stop or full-service, is familiar to those in the world of advertising agencies. Here, there has been a cycle of activity that moved away from providing everything under one roof to, during the 1970s, the emergence of specialists dealing with particular aspects of work. Now there is a move back to offering all services together, but with a general understanding that this seldom succeeds if it also attempts to embrace public relations. This view is not always shared by the chief executives of some large public relations consultancies, since it is not uncommon to find that the provision of photography, design work, publication production, sales promotion, packaging, corporate identity development and even conventional advertising is included in a consultancy's list of client services.

As with the in-house versus consultancy debate, it is pointless arguing whether such an approach is correct. The trend is that, as with so many other aspects of life, the market will decide. It is a brave chief executive who refuses the prospect of business just because the task is not classically and comprehensively public relations oriented.

The picture being drawn of public relations consultancy is that virtually all consultants are different. Not only is there vertical and horizontal segmentation and a trend towards integrated communication, but there are different structures of consultants.

At one end of the spectrum are the large international companies with offices throughout the world. Some use a common name throughout and others retain well-established 'local' brand names. The offer made by such consultants is that they are able to match the client's own international organization and provide a standard level of service throughout the world, but with adjustment to comply with any national cultural, economic or social characteristics. In other words, if a client wants a 'think global, act local' approach, such consultancies are ideally placed to respond.

Next come those consultants that are primarily concerned with one country but recognize the need for overseas connections. The development of the European Union and the speed of electronic communications has made such networks indispensable. They are provided either through an informal group of professional contacts or a more organized set-up of, for example, one independently owned consultancy in each country.

The third tier of consultancy firms are those that are much smaller – perhaps employing no more than fifteen people, and operating outside the metropolis. Included here are sole proprietor firms, limited companies and partnerships. Often they concentrate their business, perhaps on the immediate geographic area, on a particular area of practice, or on just a few clients.

The final grouping is that of independent consultant. These are individuals, usually operating from a home-based office, with very specialized talents. They can be found either working for their own clients or in association with other consultancies. Typically, they may be experienced, senior practitioners who are used to help prepare strategies, but who would be too costly to employ on a full-time basis. They might also work on an assignment basis for in-house practitioners, e.g. by managing projects.

There is no set formula to help determine whether it is better for an organization's public relations needs to be met through the services of an external consultant or by means of an internal department. There are arguments for and against each case and it is essential to consider each particular situation individually. Nevertheless, it is possible to offer some generalized points that external consultants might argue in their favour:

1   *Research*. Consultancies have the resources to dedicate an individual to providing library and research facilities. Handbooks, annuals, directories and other sources of reference material can be gathered in a library, newspapers, trade journals, consumer magazines and other periodicals received and read; and files of information and source material maintained and, increasingly, on-line databases installed to provide up-to-date media contacts and access to any array of international sources. All these services are, in the main, non-income-earning and can be expensive. However, when the cost of the overhead is spread among all clients, a research facility represents a valuable and effective part of the service offered to clients. For example, news is constantly assessed so a client's particular industry sector can be surveyed, background material to help direct new creative ideas can be accessed, and press cuttings and other media coverage can be monitored and evaluated. Such a comprehensive resource would be costly and hard to justify in any but the largest in-house department.

2   *Training*. Consultancies are able to develop structured career development plans for their executives and to provide skills training in both aspects of public relations practice as well as innovations such as 'new' media. The more progressive consultancies apply the Public Relations Education Trust's matrix to guide such training and ensure that it is related to appropriate levels of staff. This can range from programmes for newly recruited people, including graduate trainees to assisting the promotion of executives through the consultancy. Training can also include education programmes such as the CAM certificate and diploma and the degree courses that are available. Whether studied by full-time attendance at an institution or through distance learning, the support and backing of a consultancy employer, and the associated opportunities to use colleagues as professional tutors, are invaluable. It is unusual to find an in-house department, unless there are many individuals on the staff, able to provide such breadth and depth of training. Equally important, and related to training, is the opportunity for continuous professional development. While for more junior individuals the aim of education and training is to equip practitioners with the necessary intellectual and practical skills to practise, more senior consultants need to update their skills constantly and structured professional development programmes, such as that being introduced by the Institute of Public Relations, can be implemented in a consultancy.

3 *Media contacts.* Few clients or employers do not seek constant exposure in the media. Achieving this requires, apart from other professional and journalistic skills, a network of contacts. Having a good reason for making contact with the media is the only way of safeguarding the integrity of contacts, and a range of client stories enhances both the reputation of individuals and of consultancies. Therefore being able to talk to a journalist about a number of subjects from several clients helps build and reinforce contacts and benefit all clients. If there is only one 'principal', as in the case of an in-house practitioner, the opportunity for frequent contact with journalists is consequentially reduced.

4 *Other clients.* The 'spin-off' advantage of taking news about several clients to the media also applies to networking among clients. All consultancies are required to monitor their clients to avoid competition and conflict. However, complementary clients can sometimes work together. For example, if a consultant is handling a charity client, it may be relevant to suggest support for such a cause to another client where sponsorship is the solution to a public relations objective. Equally, if a packaging manufacturer is a client, knowledge gained from that sector of industry may be helpful in promoting another client in, say, the fast food business, which is concerned about environmental pollution from wrapping materials.

5 *Creativity.* This is one of the most important benefits brought to public relations practice by consultancies. There is an ever-present search for new ideas and fresh approaches to existing situations. Creativity in public relations programmes requires a spark of inspiration and a great deal of intense debate. Consultancies are able, with relative ease, to bring together a group of people who understand the principles of practice and are able to apply their collective lateral thinking to brain-storm a client brief and produce a creative response. This can only come from a group of people who have reached a certain stage in practice and who do not need to be initiated in basic processes. Finding such a group in an internal department would, again, be difficult, because there would not be, in general, sufficient individuals of sufficient status to achieve the object of the exercise.

Clearly, one of the overriding reasons to use external consultants is to provide an objective and dispassionate observer. This quality is of the greatest value in corporate public relations activity. Indeed some would argue that it is only in corporate work that such objectivity applies. While there are always exceptions and it is dangerous to claim absolute cases, it is probably true that in, for example, marketing public relations programmes for both consumer and business-to-business products, the consultant works to a rigid and closely defined brief affording little discretion. The client knows what is wanted and does not expect to receive a stream of gratuitous comment and advice on anything outside that brief. Of course there is no reason why the consultant should not seek to expand the brief and to present fresh ideas to revitalize and extend campaigns. Indeed, this is an essential activity if the consultant is to enjoy a lengthy and financially rewarding relationship with the client. Success is judged not merely on the satisfactory achievement of quantifiable objectives but also on creative innovation.

The issue of objective comment applies not only to an organization's communication needs. In fact this is only one aspect that will be relevant. To be of most value, the consultant needs to understand the activities and business of the client in the broadest possible sense. In public relations terms this will entail constant re-examination and redefinition of target audiences and the critical elements that comprise those audiences. This is a changing scene, since influences such as legislation, market conditions, economic and environmental pressure mean that the business world is dynamic. Add to this the inevitable movements of individuals as various personalities find their political, social and economic fortunes wax and wane, and the complexities become apparent. Understanding the business as a whole requires knowledge of the internal structure of the client, and an appreciation of the various functional and operational activities – of the key executives, of the different power bases, and of the ways in which both management strategy and corporate policy are decided. If this seems far removed from the classical ideals of a public relations consultant, it is not surprising. Increasingly it is necessary for the consultant to become attuned to the broad concepts and practices of management and, consequently, to be as much a management as a public relations consultant.

The inevitable development of this point of view is to look inwards towards the consultant's own business (assuming that in this case the consultancy is a reasonable substantial firm and not an independent individual). The management strands of the client organization will be replicated within the consultancy, though on a probably smaller scale. Financial controls, personnel recruitment policies, staff training and development, business development and marketing, resource management and strategic planning are all within the orbit of the consultancy. This realization has brought about a new breed of consultancy managers and an acceptance that managing a public relations consultancy requires the same skills as are needed for the management of any business.

It has in the past been regrettably true that very few chief executives of public relations consultancies in the UK were adept managers. The most brilliant public relations person was often exposed as a weak and ineffectual manager. The inevitable question to ask is how can such a person offer effective and valued objective advice to a client? Fortunately this 'physician heal thyself' syndrome is past. The whole field of public relations consultancy is entering an exciting and new stage. From the handful of public relations consultancies that have successfully achieved BS5750/ISO9000 accreditation, we can expect to see a flood. These are the businesses that have put their own systems and management practices to the test and have proved that they can function on the same management plane as their clients. They have introduced programmes of customer care and quality control they would expect to see in their client. Moreover, it is probably this type of approach that, if lacking, would have been recommended by the objective external observer.

As time progresses and both the nature of public relations changes, as does the type of support demanded by clients, the need to control and regulate the practice of public relations becomes increasing crucial. The activities of individual practitioners in the UK are controlled by the Code of Conduct of the Institute of Public Relations. Although this Code was first developed in the early days of the IPR in the late 1940s, it is an organic collection of statements and is comprehensively revised, as a matter of policy, every five years. Furthermore, there are opportunities at each annual general meeting to introduce or amend clauses in the light of changing professional practice. Naturally the Code only applies to those who recognize that claims to professionalism impose a duty to join and be bound by the professional body. This is a voluntary action, at the moment. Within the next few years – perhaps by the turn of the century – the IPR will have achieved formal recognition through a Royal Charter and then be ready for the next logical stage of statutory registration. This would be welcomed by many, since it will confound those who seek to denigrate and revile public relations practice. The charlatan publicists will be removed from the scene through legal constraints.

So far as consultancies are concerned, the trade association that regulates activity is the Public Relations Consultants Association. Formed from the IPR, this is principally concerned with commercial issues and only offers corporate membership. It too, has a code of practice, again derived from the Institute's. But, in addition, the PRCA has developed a Code of Investor Relations Practice and a Code of Practice for Healthcare Public Relations. These supplement the main Professional Charter by determining conduct in specialized areas that have in the past given cause for concern or confusion.

This is an interesting and encouraging development. It recognizes that public relations consultancies are becoming increasingly specialized and that the fields in which they practise are controlled by new regulatory processes. External consultants have to be both cognisant of those regulations and to uphold them in order to safeguard the interests of their clients.

In time it is expected that there will be further specialist codes of this nature, e.g. covering the somewhat vexed area of government lobbying. This could be an interesting development, since the House of Commons Select Committee on Members' Interests has vacillated for several years on such issues as whether it is proper for MPs to receive fees to represent particular commercial interests. By introducing its own code of conduct, it is reasonable to suppose that the public relations consultancy business will be able to demonstrate the competence and ability to regulate itself. This is the clearest possible indication that the practice of consultancy public relations has become firmly established as an indispensable element in the political, economic and commercial world.

11

Ethics and Codes of Professional Conduct

Sue Wolstenholme

According to Groucho Marx, 'The secret of life is honesty and fair dealing. If you can fake that you've got it made'.

The subject of ethics has in recent years started to move to centre stage in business and organizational studies. Perhaps with the growth of information technology it has become much more difficult to 'fake it', or, more probably, with better educated publics and more professional practised public relations it has become clear that truth and integrity are central to long-term success.

Public relations practitioners have a key role to play as maintainers of the corporate conscience and managers of reputation. Professor Melvin Sharpe has written: 'Ethical harmony is essential for social stability. And social stability is the mission and product of public relations'.[1] However, there have never been such mobile goalposts as those that frame society's ethical values.

As knowledge widens and information is capable of moving at great speed, many individuals are constantly re-evaluating positions and seeking more information on which to base their thinking. To that end public relations as a conduit for information to, from and throughout organizations must be practised with a deep appreciation and a wide knowledge of ethical propositions.

The *Public Relations Journal* ran a sub-head: 'Exploring foundational ethical values is as essential as finding our next client',[2] putting the vital need for the kind of research right at the front of public relations practice because 'potential ethical issues are inherent in any instance of communication between humans'.[3]

The need to be able to analyse ethical problems is apparent in all aspects of public relations from media relations to corporate strategy planning, and it also has a role in the professional future of public relations itself.

According to Buchholz, 'Professions psychologically and culturally legitimize themselves by their codes'... 'Operating essentially as a social contract that outlines group values, norms and responsibilities, a professional code reinforces an occupation's claims to unique social utility' [4] It is obvious that unless public relations practitioners at all levels are mindful of their *own* ethical values, they will be at a clear disadvantage when trying to create harmony between the values of clients and publics. Ethics are essentially personal and constantly under re-evaluation, so the published codes may be difficult to adapt individually.

Problems can arise if a practitioner is ordered to issue incorrect information to the media or to breach the Code of Conduct in some other way. There cannot be any compromise in such situations and a firm stand has to be taken, however difficult. Similar difficulties affect other professional practitioners. The Institute of Chartered Secretaries and Administrators (ICSA) has taken a lead by pledging its members the support of the Institute if adherence to the strict letter of the ICSA Code brings them into conflict with their employers.

Students on the European Public Relations Masters course at the College of St Mark and St John in Plymouth recently staged a mock trial at which 'public relations' was on trial charged with 'working to harm democracy in Europe'. Both the prosecution and defence quoted evidence from case studies, press cuttings and various published theories. The jury found public relations as *widely* practised guilty as charged, but as it *should be*, but is too rarely, practised, innocent and indeed a powerful force for social and democratic well-being. Public relations was put on probation and advised to study the ethical codes and to enforce them more rigidly.

The moral is that any practitioner wishing to be regarded as a true professional has a personal duty to research, understand and apply ethical values.

Rotary International has developed its Four Way Test, which is binding on all Rotarians. It poses four simple questions. Is it the truth? Is it fair to all concerned? Will it build goodwill and better friendship? Will it be beneficial to all concerned?

The importance of establishing a code of professional conduct was appreciated by the Institute of Public Relations soon after it was formed in 1948. The IPR Code of Professional Conduct has been updated regularly. The current text, which is mandatory on all members of the Institute, is included in this chapter, together with the explanatory interpretation published by the Institute.

Today increased attention is being paid to business ethics, but in public relations practice there has long been a conviction that business ethics and moral standards are an essential underpinning of good and successful business. The Institute of Public Relations (IPR) adopted its Code of

Professional Conduct in 1963 after some years of preparation to ensure that the text covered all the most important aspects of the relationships between practitioners and employers and clients, while safeguarding the integrity of the media. Many of these relationships are governed by law, but, apart from legal or contract requirements, it has become clear that truth and integrity are central to long-term success. Good reputation today can only be built on sound ethical values.

Public relations practice can only flourish in a free society, and it is always essential to take account of the 'public interest'. Codes of conduct of an association are drawn up both to provide a practical ethical framework for its members and also to send the correct professional message to the outside world.

Codes of this kind are of little practical value unless they are enforced. The IPR investigates any alleged breaches of the Code by any of its members, and if the complaint is substantiated, the member is reprimanded or may be expelled from membership. Since the IPR Code was adopted, there have been a number of instances where members have been removed from membership for serious breaches of the code.

The Institute of Public Relations
Code of Professional Conduct and Guidelines for Members
(revised July 1993)

INTRODUCTION

The Code of Professional Conduct has been drawn up by the Institute of Public Relations to set down standards which will, it is hoped, make for good relationships and reputable business dealing by public relations practitioners. There are other, internationally adopted, Codes of Conduct which have the support of the Institute.

The Code is binding on members of the Institute and is under constant review. The latest revisions were approved by the Annual General Meeting in 1991. These Guidelines should be used in conjunction with other Guidelines and Recommended Practice Papers issued by the Institute from time to time. They are intended to assist members in interpreting the Code, but it must be emphasised that they cannot be all-embracing. Circumstances vary and it is up to members to measure their conduct against the standards set by the Code.

Complaints about breaches of the Code, which may come from any individual or organization, are investigated by the Institute's Professional Practices Committee which, if considered appropriate, may refer the matter to the Disciplinary Committee for action. The Code is in no way a substitute for the law of the land, and anyone seeking redress against a member should do so through the normal legal processes.

Arbitration over a dispute is not part of the function of the Professional Practices Committee, but the Committee can sometimes appoint three senior Fellows of the Institute to act as arbitrators, provided all the parties connected with the dispute agree, in advance, to be bound by the outcome.

Nor does the Committee comment on the amount of fees charged by a member, since these are conditioned by many factors outside the Institute's control. Terms of business are usually negotiated in advance and should be adhered to.

Whilst the Committee will consider complaints about members from non-members, it is not usually able to consider complaints from members about non-members.

Clause 1: Conduct concerning the practice of public relations

A member shall:

1.1 Have a positive duty to observe the highest standards in the practice of public relations and to deal fairly and honestly with employers and clients (past and present), fellow members and professionals, the public relations profession, other professions, suppliers, intermediaries, the media of communications, employees and the public.

1.1 This clause emphasises the fact that the Code applies to a member's relationships with many different 'publics'. The list may not be comprehensive.

1.2 Be aware of, understand and observe this Code, any amendment to it, and any other codes which shall be incorporated into it; remain up to date with the content and recommendations of any guidance or practice papers issued by IPR: and have a duty to conform to good practice as expressed in such guidance or practice papers.

1.2 The Code is not a piece of window dressing; members have a positive duty to observe the Code, follow any changes that may be made to it and conform to any guidance or interpretation that may from time to time be agreed by the Institute's Council and promulgated to members.

1.3 Uphold this Code and co-operate with fellow members to enforce decisions on any matter arising from its application. A member who knowingly causes or allows his or her staff to act in a manner inconsistent with this Code is party to such action and shall be deemed to be in breach of this Code. Staff employed by a member who act in a manner inconsistent with this Code should be disciplined by the member.

1.3 Responsibility for upholding the Code and the principles it embodies does not apply solely to members' own behaviour, but also to the extent to which they can exercise influence over others, especially members of their staff and fellow members.

A member shall not:

1.4 Engage in any practice nor be seen to conduct him or her self in any manner detrimental to the reputation of the Institute or the reputation and interests of the public relations profession.

1.4 This is a 'catch-all' clause. If, for example, a member is seen to be drunk or found to be dishonest, such behaviour may be detrimental to the Institute or the public relations profession. Whether such behaviour is actually in breach of this clause would have to be judged on the particular circumstances of the case.

Clause 2: Conduct concerning the public, the media and other professionals

A member shall:

2.1 Conduct his or her professional activities with proper regard to the public interest.

2.1 Emphasises the importance of responsible behaviour by public relations practitioners. The public interest is not easy to define; a product may be in the interests of one section of the public but contrary to the interests of another. The Code calls for a responsible attitude to all sections of the public.

2.2 Have a positive duty at all times to respect the truth and shall not disseminate false or misleading information knowingly or recklessly, and take proper care to check all information prior to its dissemination.

2.2 It is worth emphasising that this clause applies whether the member is an employer or an employee.

2.3 Have a duty to ensure that the actual interest of any organisation with which he or she may be professionally concerned is adequately declared.

2.3 A member representing a client or employer must make the client's interest known when making representations and in a manner which is straightforward and does not mislead. The use of a 'front' organisation or name suggesting an objective different from that of a member's client or employer is not permitted. (E.g. A hypothetical 'Paint Advisory Service' whose title would suggest the availability of 'neutral' advice on any paint problem, but whose ultimate objective is the sale of a particular make of paint.)

2.4 When working in association with other professionals, identify and respect the codes of those professions.

2.4 Public relations work is not done in isolation as is the case with some professions. A member may be working closely with, for example, a journalist, accountant or lawyer and must take care that they or their profession are in no way compromised.

2.5 Respect any statutory or regulatory codes laid down by any other authorities which are relevant to the actions of his or her employer or client, or taken on behalf of an employer or client.

2.5 This is a warning about the many regulations or codes, voluntary and statutory, that may be relevant to an intended course of action. Where appropriate members should familiarise themselves with these regulations and not only avoid offending against them, but should warn their employer or client against so doing.

2.6 Ensure that the names of all directors, executives, and retained advisers of his or her employers or company who hold public office, are members of either House of Parliament, Local Authorities or of any statutory organisation or body, are recorded in the IPR Register.

2.6 Members have a positive duty to declare, in the register, any public office-holder retained by them or their employers. The register is maintained by the Institute and is available to members or non-members on request.

2.7 Honour confidences received or given in the course of professional activity.

2.7 Members can only work effectively if they have the confidence of their client or employer. This clause emphasises that respecting such confidence is a professional duty and applies even if the connection with that employer or client has ended.

2.8 Neither propose nor undertake, or cause an employer or client to propose or undertake, any action which would be an improper influence on government, legislation, holders of public office or members of any statutory body or organisation, or the media of communication.

2.8 The purpose of public relations is to promote better mutual understanding and this should be the keynote in trying to impress on the media or on representatives of the government, local authorities or other organisations, any need to effect changes in the law or the rules laid down by such organizations.

It is for individual members to judge whether payments, gifts or other 'inducements' given to holders of public office other than those declared under 2.6, are in contravention of this clause. Though, in the event of a complaint, such judgement would fall to the Professional Practices Committee.

Clause 3: Conduct concerning employers and clients

A member shall:

3.1 Safeguard the confidences of both present and former employers or clients: shall not disclose or use these confidences to the disadvantage or prejudice of such employers or clients, or to the financial advantage of the member (unless the employer or client has released such information for public use, or has given specific permission for disclosure), except upon the order of a court of law.

3.1 This is an extension to clause 2.7, applying specifically to confidential information gained from past or present clients or employers. For example: a member may not give confidential information about one client to a competitor of the client, or provide information about a client to a third party in return for some sort of reward. There are various other ways in which this clause could be contravened, but the clause could be over-ruled by a Court of Law.

3.2 Inform an employer or client of any shareholding or financial interest held by that member or any staff employed by that member in any company or person whose services he or she recommends.

3.2 This safeguards employers or clients from possible undisclosed interests a member may have when recommending the use of a third party.

3.3 Be free to accept fees, commissions or other valuable considerations from persons other than an employer or client, if such considerations are disclosed to the employer or client.

3.3 This permits, for example, a percentage of printing costs being taken by a member, but only if this is disclosed to the client or employer. Although not specifically stated, it is implied in the Code that this disclosure should be at the time fees are agreed.

3.4 Be free to negotiate, or renegotiate, with an employer or client terms that are a fair reflection of demands of the work involved and take into account factors ôther than hours worked and the experience involved. These special factors, which are also applied by other professional advisers, shall have regard to all the circumstances of the specific situation and in particular to:
a) The complexity of the issue, case, problem or assignment, and the difficulties associated with its completion.
b) The professional or specialised skills required and the degree of responsibility involved.
c) The amount of documentation necessary to be perused or prepared, and its importance.
d) The place and circumstances where the work is carried out, in whole or in part.
e) The scope, scale and value of the task and its importance as an activity, issue or project to the employer or client.

3.4 Public relations work varies greatly in complexity and this clause sets out five factors to be taken into account in negotiating fee or salary. There may well be others. If, during the course of an assignment circumstances change a re-negotiation could be in order.

A member shall not:

3.5 Misuse information regarding his or her employer's or client's business for financial or other gain.

3.5 This clause refers to the misuse of any information about an employer's or client's business, to a member's advantage whether or not the information is confidential.

3.6 Use inside information for gain. Nor may a member of staff managed or employed by a member directly trade in his or her employer's or client's securities without the prior written permission of the employer or client and of the member's chief executive or chief financial officer or compliance officer.

3.6 'Inside information' is information about an employer or client obtained during the course of a member's employment which would not be fully available to outsiders. The clause applies particularly to information concerning the financial status of the company concerned. Statutory and regulatory provisions place strict conditions on the conduct of financial communications and on trading in the company's shares or other securities as required by the Stock Exchange's listing requirements.

3.7 Serve an employer or client under terms or conditions which might impair his or her independence, objectivity or integrity.

3.7 This clause is designed to protect members from unfair conditions being imposed that might impair their judgement or compromise their integrity. For example, members should not accept a condition seeking to cause them to publish false information, thus breaching clause 2.2.

3.8 Represent conflicting interests but may represent competing interests with the express consent of the parties concerned.

3.8 Example: It would be a breach to represent both Coca Cola and Pepsi Cola, but provided both parties agreed, a member might represent one of them and also a brewer or a retailer. If a member is in doubt about the possibility of two clients being in conflict, the clients' views should be sought before agreeing to represent them.

3.9 Guarantee the achievement of results which are beyond the member's direct capacity to achieve or prevent.

3.9 In most of the campaigns which a public relations practitioner undertakes, the outcome is influenced by a number of factors only partially or not at all under the control of the practitioner:

For example, a member acting for a company making a hostile bid for another would be quite wrong to guarantee success. Similarly it would be wrong to guarantee a specific amount of favourable press coverage.

Clause 4: Conduct concerning colleagues

A member shall:

4.1 Adhere to the highest standards of accuracy and truth, avoiding extravagant claims or unfair comparisons and giving credit for ideas and words borrowed from others.

4.1 All public relations work is concerned with ideas, which may come from various sources. Practitioners naturally want to lay claim to their successes, but must stick to the truth in doing so, give credit where it is due and not plagiarise other people's ideas.

4.2 Be free to represent his or her capabilities and service to any potential employer or client, either on his or her own initiative or at the behest of any client, provided in so doing he or she does not seek to break any existing contract or detract from the reputation or capabilities of any member already serving that employer or client.

4.2 A member is, of course, free to seek new clients or a new employer, but in doing so must not in any way denigrate another member, who may be already working for the prospective client or employer. If a member is making a presentation to a prospective client it is usual and courteous to inform any existing member concerned, or at least to ask the 'prospect' to ignore the approach where public relations needs are already being satisfactorily met.

A member shall not:

4.3 Injure the professional reputation or practice of another member.

4.3 This clause scarcely calls for further comment. It is not difficult to damage a person's or a corporation's professional reputation. To do so where a fellow member is concerned would contravene the Code if not the libel laws.

Clause 5: Interpreting the code

5.1 In the interpretation of this code, the Laws of the Land shall apply.

5.1 Even the IPR Code is not above the law!

Other codes of professional conduct

Most of the national public relations associations have codes of professional conduct that are comparable to the IPR Code but may differ in detail.

The Public Relations Society of America (PRSA) has a very strict code. It is enforced by legal procedures set out in the code.

The Code of Athens

Both the International Public Relations Association (IPRA) and the European Confederation of Public Relations (CERP) adopted in 1965 a strict moral code based on the United Nations Declaration of Human Rights. Both associations also have their own code of professional conduct governing relations with clients, employers, the media, the public and colleagues.

Both IPRA and CERP have codes of professional conduct that complement the Code of Athens.

References

1 M Sharpe (1990) Harmonising Ethical Values in the Global Village, *International Public Relations Review*, Vol. 13, No 3, p. 25.

2 J Jurgensen and J Lukaszewski (1988) Ethics: contents before conduct, *Public Relations Journal*, March, p. 47.

3 R Johannessen (1983) *Ethics in Human Communication*, 2nd Edition, Waveland Press, Illinois, p. 1.

4 W Buchholz (1989) Deciphering Professional Codes of Ethics, *IEEE Transactions on Professional Communication*, Vol. 32, No 2, June, p. 62.

12

Legal aspects of public relations practice

Mark D Grundy

You do not have to be a lawyer to be a good public relations person, but some knowledge of the law will help you to be a better one. There are three reasons for this:

1 The practice of public relations, like any other profession or business, has to be carried out within its own legal context covering both contractual relationships and public law.
2 In advising clients or employers, public relations practitioners will often be concerned with 'legal' situations. A factory is being closed – what is the law on redundancy? A share issue is to be made – what are the legal requirements on disclosure? No matter that these are the responsibility of clients and their lawyers; public relations advisers are at a disadvantage unless they themselves know (or know how to find) the elements of the law on such matters. At least they will then be able to give advice that is within the limits of practicability, and be able to 'speak the same language' as their fellow-advisers of other professions. At most they may find increased opportunities for public relations initiatives.
3 The logical analysis of problems and situations used by lawyers can be an extremely useful discipline for the public relations practitioner. However creative the thought put into a public relations programme, it will be convincing in proportion to the degree of orderly thought and clarity of expression with which it is presented.

The law of England and Wales (with which for most purposes goes the law of Northern Ireland) is different in a number of ways from Scottish law. Scotland has its own legal profession and its own law courts; it jealously guards its own legal traditions, which, like those of Continental countries, have their roots in Roman Law. We will deal here basically with English law, pointing out some of the difficulties in Scotland.

There is of course a basic distinction between criminal law (matters punishable as offences) and civil law (matters that can be the subject of legal claims by one person or organization against another). Here we shall mainly be concerned with civil law, though certain areas such as consumer protection and employee protection may lead to either civil claims or criminal prosecutions, or both.

The rest of this chapter is intended to give a bird's eye view of some widely relevant aspects. More specialized fields cannot be covered, but may seem less daunting when general principles are known.

Contracts

A contract is a legally binding agreement. It does not have to be in the form of a written document and can be verbal or implied by actions such as a purchase in a shop.

Probably the two types of contract that most concern public relations people professionally are contracts with suppliers and contracts of employment. It is surprisingly common in our profession for these types of contract to be made informally, or even verbally. There is a tendency to feel that to use anything like a legal document indicates a rigid, unfriendly attitude, and suggests one party is seeking to 'pin down' the other for his/her own advantage. While it is often unnecessary to use a document in legal phraseology, if you do not do so, you must accept a more difficult task in ensuring you state precisely what has been agreed. As we all know, the time when this matters is when something goes wrong, and then it is too late.

To be legally binding, a simple contract must:

1   Be intended to create legal relations (and be capable of doing so). An agreement for a lunch date, for example, is not normally an enforceable contract!
2   Made by people who have legal capacity to contract (a minor cannot make certain types of contract; employees cannot bind their company by contract unless they are authorized to do so, and so on).
3   Be based on an agreement between two or more parties, reached by an offer and an acceptance of that offer.
4   Be supported by 'consideration' (except in the case of a deed). This means that something of value – however small, and not necessarily in money or goods – must pass from each party to the other.

Agreement

An agreement may be express or implied. In either case there must be an offer on one side and acceptance on the other.

An offer must be distinguished from an invitation to make an offer. If a consultancy advertises its services, it is merely inviting potential clients to offer an assignment. If a company advertises a job, it is merely inviting potential employees to apply. The consultancy need not take an assignment offered to it, and the company need not employ an applicant. Only when an actual offer is made and accepted – when the parties are agreed – is there actually a contact.

At the same time, an offer need not be made to a specific person. It can be made to people in general and accepted by an individual.

Even when an offer is made, it can be revoked at any time before it has been accepted. The acceptance must have been communicated to you before you withdraw (the law presumes that where acceptance is contemplated by post, acceptance is made when the letter of acceptance is posted).

For an agreement to be binding, the parties must be at one on all essential points, so it is sensible to spell out these points clearly in writing and ensure that the person with whom you are contracting accepts them. If you are ordering artwork, for instance, make it clear whether you wish to buy the copyright, or merely the right to reproduce on a single occasion – or just the physical drawing or painting.

Consideration

You can enforce a contract (other than a deed) at law only if you can show that you have provided some 'consideration'. This need not take the form of payment. It can be any benefit you provide to the other party, or something you agree to give up or forgo: the value need not be sufficient or adequate. In many cases the consideration will be a promise to do something (employ a person, supply goods or services, for example) in exchange for another promise (to work for the employer, pay for the goods or services).

Acceptance can, however, be implied. If you allow employees to start work without making a specific agreement to employ them, you will be bound by implication to pay them for what they do.

Terms

The terms of a contact, like the offer and acceptance, may be written, oral or implied. If they are broken by either side, the aggrieved party can sue for damages, and if they go to the root of the agreement, he/she can claim that the contract is at an end.

In the case of an agreement for public relations consultancy it obviously avoids problems if the parties contract on the basis of detailed written terms or conditions. (The Public Relations Consultants Association provides model terms for inclusion in consultancy contracts, and CERP, the European Public Relations Confederation, supplies a model form of agreement.) Such terms, including such matters as notice periods, payment of out-of-pocket expenses, and indemnity against claims by third parties, can either be part of a formal contract or 'built in' to a contract made by letter, so long as it is made quite clear that they are to be regarded as part of the agreement, and accepted as such. Suppliers or consultants may print such terms or conditions on their order form, and if the order is accepted, the contract will be on the basis of those conditions, unless there is any agreement to the contrary.

Where a term of the contract is not covered by written 'conditions', it may be implied by law or by the custom of the trade. Long before modern consumer protection legislation, the Sale of Goods Act 1893 (now the Sale of Goods Act 1979) established basic implied terms for sale of goods. The Act covers three principal points:

1 Sale by description, where goods must correspond with the description.
2 Condition of fitness for the purpose for which goods are normally intended.
3 Merchantable quality, i.e. that goods are basically of a quality that is suitable for those goods.

Human nature being what it is, people or companies making contracts will attempt to by-pass legal restrictions by 'contracting-out' of them if they can. Two Acts stopped up loopholes of this kind. The Supply of Goods (Implied Terms) Act 1973 prohibited contracting out of the conditions on description, 'merchantability' and fitness in sales to consumers. The Unfair Contract Terms Act 1977 made illegal, in certain circumstances, unreasonable exemption clauses seeking to exclude liability by one party to the other.

Mistake

If a party to a contract entered the agreement under a mistake of fact on an essential matter, the contract will be held void, simply because the offer and acceptance did not correspond.

It is common sense to read, and make sure you understand, a written contract before you sign it. Normally you will be bound by the terms of the contract even if you have not read it.

Misrepresentation

A 'representation' is a statement made by one person that induces another to enter a contract with him/her. If the statement is false – a 'misrepresentation' – the law will provide a remedy for the party that has acted on it to his/her detriment.

The familiar rule *caveat emptor* – 'let the buyer beware' – lives on, even though much modified by recent legislation. Under the general law no one is bound to make any 'representation' at all. Sellers do not have to tell buyers of defects in the article they are selling; it is up to buyers to find out. But if they are asked, or choose to describe the goods, they must be truthful, or they will be liable for the result of their misrepresentation. This is so even if the statement was true when they made it, but later became false. Suppose that you, as a consultant, tell a potential client that his/her account will be handled by a highly skilled member of your staff. That member of your staff leaves, but you enter a contract with the client without disclosing the changed situation. If the client was led to make the contract on the basis of your representation, he/she would have a valid claim against you.

Misrepresentation may of course be either fraudulent or innocent. In either case the injured party may choose to set aside the contract, or to sue for damages; but if the defendant can show that he/she believed on reasonable grounds *up to the time of the contract* that the statement was true, he/she can escape damages.

There are various situations where disclosure is specifically required. Apart from modern consumer protection law, the commonest example is that of insurance; if the party seeking to be insured does not disclose all material facts, the insurer can rescind the contract. Contracts between partners likewise require full disclosure.

Contracts in restraint of trade

Certain types of contract are by their nature illegal and, consequently, unenforceable. One of the most important of these is the contract 'in restraint of trade', because it can often apply to employment situations. In contracts for senior and specialist posts employers often wish to impose restrictions on employees even after they have left the company. A consultancy, for instance, may wish to include a term in its directors' contracts binding them not to approach the firm's clients for some fixed period after the director has left the firm. To be upheld by the courts, a restriction like this must be shown to be reasonably necessary to protect the interests of the employer, and not unreasonable as regards the employee or the public. (The length of period will be one of the factors taken into account here; the extent of the restrictions will be another.) Contracts of this kind that do not meet these conditions are held illegal, as being 'in restraint of trade' and therefore contrary to public policy, though if a contract is valid apart from the restrictive clause, the remainder will be enforced.

How does a contract come to an end?

There are six ways in which a valid contract comes to an end:

1 Expiry of time – this need not be a fixed term but can continue until the expiry of notice.
2 Performance – when a specific job has been carried out.
3 Agreement – if both parties wish to end (or change) the contract, they can agree to do so.
4 By operation of law. A contract for personal services, for example, ends with the death of either party.
5 Frustration. If circumstances have changed radically so that the contract cannot be performed in its original form, it is at an end.
6 Breach of contract. If a contract is broken in such a way that it is useless or unfair to the other party to continue it, it may be terminated.

A 'simple' contract can be enforced by legal action only up to six years after the contract is entered into; a contract by deed is enforceable up to twelve years. These are periods to remember when destroying letters, invoices or other papers that could be evidence in any dispute. (However, if the debtor acknowledges his/her debt in writing or makes part payment, the time starts to run again from the date of these events.)

Remedies for breach

If a breach of contract occurs, the other party can, as an alternative or in addition to suing for damages, ask the court to order the party in breach to carry out his/her agreement. He/she can also ask for an injunction to prevent further breaches.

Assignment

The benefits of a contract can be assigned to a third party, under certain conditions, but not the liabilities. You can, for instance, assign the fees you receive for your public relations work but you cannot (without first agreeing with the client) assign the legal responsibility of carrying out the work to another consultant or firm. You may be able to sub-contract, but this will depend on the terms of the contract, stated or implied.

Careless misstatement

Any contract for the provision of advice, say by a public relations consultant, has an implied duty of care owed to the client, unless that condition is expressly excluded or limited. Even where there is no contract, professional people owe a duty of care to people who can be expected to rely upon their skill.

It was made clear in the important *Hedley Byrne* case in 1964 that this duty of reasonable care extends to voluntary statements made by anyone to someone else who can be expected to rely on their truth, unless liability is expressly excluded. The most obvious example of this is where, as in the Hedley Byrne case itself, a misleading reference is given. There is no obligation to give a reference, e.g. on an employee or a business, at all; but if you do so, you must take reasonable care that it is accurate and sufficiently complete. You can, however, exclude liability by stating specifically that you give the reference 'without responsibility'.

Agency and vicarious liability

An aspect of the law that is often of great importance to professional people such as public relations practitioners is how far one is responsible in law for someone else's act. The rules on this differ according to whether we are considering contracts, torts (civil wrongs based on contract) or criminal offences.

Agency

An agent is a person given authority by another (called the principal) to do something on his/her behalf, such as enter a contract.

In public relations consultancy it is important, for reasons that will appear, to be clear about when consultants are acting directly and when they are acting as agents for their clients. The point arises whenever, for instance, they book a room for a press conference or order printwork in the course of their assignment.

If consultants are acting as principals, the buck stops with them. Any claim by suppliers for payment, etc., can only be made against them, and whether or not they can recover from their clients is their problem, not the suppliers'. If the consultant is openly acting as the client's agent, the supplier must normally claim against the client (the consultant's principal) and not against the consultant; moreover, only the client can sue the supplier if necessary. If, however, the consultant has not disclosed the fact that he/she is acting as agent, the supplier can claim against the consultant, though provided he/she has acted within the client's actual authority, the client must indemnify the consultancy.

The agency situation can arise merely by implication. If clients put the consultants in a position where they appear to the third party to have authority to act for them, they cannot afterwards deny that they were so authorized (even if, for instance, unknown to the suppliers they had forbidden the consultants to place the order).

It is important to note that it is a criminal offence, under the Prevention of Corruption Act 1906, for an agent to take any undisclosed commission or other reward in connection with the client's business. An agent that makes any undisclosed profit can be sued in the civil courts and made to hand it over.

Generally it is more satisfactory, in a public relations consultancy, for the consultant to make it clear to all parties that he/she is acting as principal, and recharge the client as necessary. For this reason, it is sensible to avoid referring to a public relations 'agency' or 'agent', as this could lead to legal problems.

Vicarious liability – tort

Employers are liable for torts committed by their employees or agents in the course of their employment. This means that if a member of your staff is, for example, negligent, causing damage to a third party, *you* can be sued as well as the employee. This liability arises only if the tort was committed in the course of employment; the courts interpret this quite widely, and the test is really whether employees were doing what they were employed to do – even if, as will usually be the case, the employers would not have wished them to carry out their duties in a harmful way. We have taken negligence as an example, but the same rule applies to all torts, including, for instance, defamation or passing off.

This 'vicarious liability' applies in the case of employees, but not normally in the case of an independent contractor. The important difference is that employees are subject to the employer's control, not only on what they do, but how they are to do it: the fact that they disobey their instructions is unfortunately irrelevant, unless they go 'on a frolic of their own'.

Employers are liable for the torts of an independent contractor only if they have chosen the contractor negligently, or if they have given instructions not only on what work is to be done but how it is to be done, or otherwise interfered – in effect assuming the sort of control they are presumed to have over an employee. An independent contractor, by definition, has a contract to perform *services*, as distinct from the contract of *service*, which creates the relationship of employer and employee with the control that that implies.

Vicarious liability – criminal offences

If employees commit a criminal offence, the basic rule is that employers are not liable, even if the offence is committed in the course of employment, unless it is done on their instructions, or with their assistance. This rule, however, is subject to certain exceptions arising from Acts such as offences relating to the sale of food and drugs.

Employment law

Trade unions

Provisions on trade unions' membership are contained in the Employment Protection (Consolidation) Act 1978 and the Employment Act 1982. The requirements for disclosure of certain information to unions contained in this statute can be of relevance to public – especially internal – relations.

Contracts of employment

We have seen the distinction between a contract for services (such as a consultancy agreement or a contract with a freelance) and a contract for service, i.e. employment (between employer and employee). Contracts of employment basically follow the same rules as contracts in general, but are affected by special legislation. Although a contract of employment can be implied (the employee working, the employer paying wages), or merely verbal, the Trade Unions Reform Employment Rights Act 1993 requires the employer to give any employee working eight hours or more per week written particulars of employment within two months of starting work. These must comprise certain specific items, including the date on which 'continuous employment' began – a matter relevant to such claims as those for unfair dismissal, maternity rights and redundancy compensation.

Action for *wrongful* dismissal has always been possible, because it amounts to breach of contract by the employer. *Unfair* dismissal is a new and fairly specific concept introduced by statute in 1971, and is the subject of hearings by industrial tribunals, which have developed a large case law of their own, and deal with a variety of matters contained in recent statutes, all of which can be important in public relations: the Equal Pay Act 1970, Trade Union and Labour Relations Act 1974, Sex Discrimination Act 1975, Employment Protection (Consolidation) Act 1978, Employment Act 1982, and Trade Union Reform Employment Rights Act 1993.

In addition to all these Acts, which it would be impossible to summarize here, the Health and Safety at Work, etc. Act 1974 is of importance to many public relations people. So, of course, is the Race Relations Act 1976. Codes of practice issued under various Acts, especially those produced by ACAS (the Arbitration, Conciliation and Advisory Service), do not have direct legal effect, but their terms may be taken into consideration, particularly by tribunals.

Companies and related matters

The financial public relations specialist needs to be familiar with company law in technical detail, but the general principles are straightforward and important to all practitioners.

The underlying concept of company law is that of the corporation. A corporation, in legal terminology, means simply a collection of persons that has a legal existence, rights and duties of its own. It is a legal 'person', quite separate from the individuals of which it is composed.

What is a company?

A company is an association of persons formed for the purpose of some business or understanding carried on in a corporate name, and incorporated by law. To carry on its business, every company needs money – its capital – provided by its members, each of whom in the normal case holds one or more shares in the enterprise, in proportion to the amount they have subscribed. The money subscribed for those shares cannot by law be repaid until the company is wound up, because it must be kept to meet any debts the company may incur, but the shares may be sold by members who wish to realize their investment. The company, being a separate legal entity, can own property in its own name, sue or be sued, owe money or be owed it by others, and even be convicted of certain criminal offences.

A group of persons formed for the purpose of trading would, without further formalities, be simply a partnership in the eys of the law. Each of its members would be fully liable for the debts of the group, as partners are. By taking the formal steps to become incorporated under the Companies Act as a company limited by shares, the group gains a very considerable advantage: the liability of each member is then restricted to the amount of his/her shares. This is the normal form of business company in Britain, but there are also certain other specialized forms of company. One is the company limited by guarantee, but not by shares: a form often used for associations that are not primarily trading bodies. The Institute of Public Relations is an example. Members of the Institute do not hold shares, but if the IPR were to be dissolved, each member would be liable to outsiders for a maximum of £5 (the sum set by its Memorandum of Association). It is also possible, but unusual, to have an *un*limited company, in which the liability of members is not limited.

The law on companies in the United Kingdom is contained in the Companies Act 1985, as amended by Companies Act 1989.

There are two main types of limited company: the private company and the public company. A public company must have at least two members. A private company need only have just one. Both these companies of either type must have at least one director and a secretary. It may have as many more members or directors as it wishes. A private company must not offer its shares or debentures to the public, whereas a public company may (but need not) do so. A public company must end its name with the words 'Public Limited Company' (instead of just 'Limited'), or the equivalent in Welsh.

Forming a company

To form a company, certain documents – notably a Memorandum of Association and Articles of Association – must be submitted to the Registrar of Companies in Cardiff for companies incorporated in England and Wales, or his/her opposite numbers in Edinburgh or Belfast. Even before this, the name of the new company will have been chosen and such name must not be too similar to that of an existing unconnected company, and certain other types of name, considered undesirable or misleading (such as those using the word 'Royal' or even 'British'), be chosen. Basic rules on company names are referred to in Part I of the Companies Act 1985.

The Memorandum and Articles together form the constitution of the company, and, once settled, can be altered only upon certain limited grounds by a general meeting of the company. Once the Memorandum and Articles, and other documentation, have been approved and fees paid, the Registrar issues a certificate of incorporation and the company may commence business.

Every company is required to make an annual return to the Registrar, which, together with the Memorandum and Articles, may be inspected at the Companies Registry offices (nowadays on microfiche).

The Companies Act 1985, as amended by the Companies Act 1989, sets out the company accounts and directors' report.

Dividends are paid to shareholders in proportion to the nominal value of their shares. Shareholders cannot insist on the payment of a dividend, unless fraud is involved, but once a dividend has been declared, its payment can be enforced like any other debt. Every trading company has an implied power to borrow and give security for the loan, unless prohibited by its Memorandum and Articles, and the issue of debentures is a frequent method used. Interest on debentures must be paid before any dividend, and debentures, unlike shares, may be redeemable. They are usually secured on the company's assets.

Directors are appointed by the members (shareholders) of a company, and can be removed by them. They need not necessarily be shareholders themselves, but their powers and duties are considerable, governed by law and by the company's Memorandum and Articles.

Two points on company meetings useful to the public relations practitioner are worth mentioning here, if only because they are seldom mentioned. The first is that the press and public may be admitted to a general meeting, and, in the case of a public company, normally are; but the decision whether they shall remain is entirely one for the meeting itself, and, if necessary, a vote is taken. Second, a speech by a shareholder defamatory of the directors has qualified privilege provided it is on a matter affecting the interests of the shareholders, but if the shareholder expressly invited the public or press to be present, he/she forfeits the privilege.

Company letterheadings, etc.

Certain information must, by virtue of Section 351 of the Companies Act 1985, appear on the company letterhead and trade literature. The registered number of the company must be given, the place of registration, and the address of the registered office. The words 'Limited' or 'Public Limited Company' must form part of the title of a limited company and be shown as such (apart from rare exceptions, and even then the fact that liability is limited must still be stated). Under Section 305 there is no need normally to give the names of directors on stationery, but if one name goes in, they all have to. Breach of these provisions is a criminal offence, and designers have to live with them!

Dissolution of companies

Dissolution of a company may be carried out in several ways. If a company has been inactive for some time, the Registrar of Companies may, after giving an opportunity to the company to object, simply strike it from the register. Apart from this, dissolution takes the form of 'winding up', which may be either compulsory or voluntary, depending whether the company is insolvent or solvent. The law was considerably tightened up by the

Insolvency Act 1985, and in certain circumstances directors who have engaged in 'wrongful trading' can be disqualified.

Partnership

Most of the law on partnerships is set out in the Partnership Act 1890, which defines a partnership simply as the 'relationship which subsists between persons carrying on a business in common with a view of profit'. So a partnership may be implied by the law, or set out in a formal agreement. There is no legal maximum number of partners. Companies may be partners, but the partnership itself is not a 'person' or corporate entity. The basic rule is that each partner is individually liable for the whole debts of the partnership without limit, though there are exceptions to this.

Defamation: libel and slander

It is an obvious fact that attacks on people's good names are the opposite of good public relations, especially since an action for defamation can be very costly, even if you are a successful defendant. National newspapers employ lawyers to read in proof every word that is printed, to avoid legal trouble before it starts. Public relations people have to do it themselves. So a knowledge of this branch of the law is vital.

Defamation has been defined as the publication of a statement that tends to lower a person in the estimation of right-thinking members of society generally, or tends to make them shun or avoid that person. English law divides defamation into libel, which covers statements in written or other permanent form, and slander, covering statements that are spoken or otherwise transitory. The rules on these two broad classes are slightly different. In Scottish law there is no distinction.

English law presumes that a libel causes damage – an action can be brought without the need to prove any quantified damage. Not so in the case of slander, where special damage must be proved except in certain definite instances.

Recognizing a libel or slander

How can you recognize a libel or slander? Four elements must always be present:

1 A defamatory statement.
2 A statement that is false (*but* the law presumes falsity until the contrary is proved).

3   A statement that is understood to refer to the plaintiff.
4   One that has been published (made known) to a third party.

Clearly there are all sorts of ways in which a statement can be defamatory, within the definition given earlier. Apart from the obvious ones, such as implication that the person concerned is in financial difficulties, has committed an offence, or is dishonest or immoral, the law has held that it is defamatory to say that someone is insane (if he/she is not), or suffering from some unpleasant disease (if he/she is not), because these things would tend to cause him/her to be 'shunned or avoided' by other people.

At this point we must mention 'innuendo', a word with a specific legal meaning. A statement that on the face of it is not defamatory may be so by innuendo, i.e. in the light of knowledge possessed by the third party to whom it is published. In a famous case an advertisement for chocolate featuring a star golfer was held defamatory because people who knew the golfer was an amateur would believe he had given permission in return for a cash payment, which in fact he had not.

We have mentioned that the law presumes a statement claimed as defamatory to be false unless proved otherwise. The point here is that *proving* the truth of something in court is not always easy. The statement must be understood to refer to the plaintiff even if it was not intended to do so. Unlike in some other countries, civil law in Britain does not provide a remedy for libel on a large class of people (such as Catholics, Communists, or tax-collectors). Anyone can say with impunity 'all public relations people are dishonest', but if a similar statement were made about 'all directors of X company', any one of those directors could sue, because they are clearly identifiable individuals whose reputation has been attacked.

Finally, there is the question of publication. This, too, has a legal meaning: the statement must have been communicated to at least one other person other than the plaintiff or his or her spouse. The person to whom the statement is published must be in a position to understand its defamatory nature.

A moment's thought will show that a defamatory statement can be published in all sorts of ways, and, once made, it is not so easy to stop it. A press release containing a defamatory statement is sent to a news agency (publication 1), which then sends it to a newspaper (publication 2), which then prints it and sells the newspaper (publication 3). Each person or firm along this chain can be sued by the defamed person, though there is a legal let-out for the luckless newsagent who sells the paper, provided he has no knowledge that it contains a libel and could not be expected to know that this was the case. A defamatory speech is heard by an audience, broadcast, reported, and so on – a similar chain of publications and resulting liability. Publication can even be unintentional: a libel on a postcard is presumed to be published, because it can be read while it travels by post.

The defences to an action for defamation are:

1 *Assent.* If the plaintiff has agreed, directly or by implication, to publication of a statement about him/herself that is true on the face of it, the defendant is not liable.
2 *Unintentional defamation,* under the Defamation Act 1952. The 1952 Act provides that if the defendant can show that he/she published the words innocently, offers to publish a reasonable correction and apology, and pays the plaintiff costs, he/she is not liable for damages. This applies when *either* the defendant did not intend the statement to refer to the plaintiff, *or* it was not defamatory on the face of it and he/she did not know it could have a defamatory meaning. Reasonable care must have been taken in either case.
3 *Justification* – i.e. truth. The law will not protect an undeserved reputation, so if the defendant can prove that the statement he/she has made is true, he/she will not be liable. Proving the truth in court is often far from easy, and the statement (including any hidden meaning) must be proved true in substance. Merely to prove that it is a correct report of someone else's statement (except in some special cases, which are privileged) is not enough.
4 *Fair comment.* If the statement is fair comment (not factual but.based on facts) on a matter of public interest, the defendant is not liable.
5 *Privilege.* This covers certain specified circumstances in which the law allows defamatory statements to be made without liability. Privilege comes in two kinds: absolute and qualified. Absolute privilege provides complete immunity in certain limited situations, such as statements made in Parliament or parliamentary papers, or in the course of judicial proceedings. Qualified privilege gives exemption in a number of other situations, *provided* the statement as to what is said and the means by which it is said is made honestly. Fair and accurate reports of parliamentary proceedings or judicial proceedings open to the public come into this category. Certain other newspapers or broadcast reports have qualified privilege subject to the publication of explanation and contradiction: among these are reports of the findings of professional bodies in relation to their members (the IPR Council, for example). Qualified privilege also attaches to a statement made by a person who had a duty to make it to another person with a corresponding interest to receive it; examples are the giving of references on former employees, and legitimate complaints

to people in authority. Qualified privilege is valid only if there is no question of malice or spite. If you issue a defamatory statement on behalf of your client of employer, it is 'his/her' privilege that normally counts. If the client is actuated by malice, you are liable as much as he/she is, even though you have acted innocently – though of course you may be able to claim against the client in turn.

In addition to damages, a plaintiff in a defamation case can also seek an injunction, temporary or permanent, to stop further publication.

In rare circumstances libel can be a criminal offence. Different conditions then apply. Truth is no defence, unless the statement can be shown to be in the public interest.

Injurious falsehood

Included in this term are slander of title, slander of goods and false statements damaging to someone's trade or business.

Defamation is essentially an attack on someone's personal reputation. Equally damaging, if not more so, can be statements that harm a business or other material interests. Under certain conditions such statements, whether oral or in writing, are actionable. The statement must be made to some person other than the plaintiff, and there must be some indirect, dishonest or other improper motive. Recklessness may qualify, but not mere carelessness.

To say that your (or your client's or employer's) goods are better than those of someone else is not actionable as slander of goods, though consumer legislation may of course apply. It is important, however, to be as alert to avoiding slander of title or of goods as ordinary defamation, and to consider the possible effect of any statement you make, especially in writing. For instance, to state falsely that a firm is no longer in existence, or no longer trading, can clearly harm the firm concerned, and could be actionable.

Copyright, registered designs and patents

Anyone concerned with public relations, communications, or any other activity with a creative element, will at some stage need to know how far the law will protect the results of his/her creative thought from being pirated by others. Except in the case of patents, the law does not protect *ideas*. It can only protect the expression of those ideas in written, artistic or other form. It is very easy for legal rights to be lost, on the one hand, or infringed, on the other, by default. Alertness pays.

Copyright

This is the most widely applicable form of protecting original work, and the most frequently misunderstood. It is governed by the Copyright Designs and Patents Act 1988, and internationally by the Universal Copyright Convention of 1952.

Copyright means the right, for a stated period, to prevent any other person (without permission of the copyright owner) from copying or using in various other ways the work concerned.

In Britain copyright exists automatically (there is no requirement or provision for registration) in, for all practical purposes, every original literary, dramatic, artistic or musical work. The word 'original' in this sense means simply that the work must have been created by the author, not copied from someone else's work: if two people produce a virtually identical drawing quite independently, each drawing will have copyright. Because, as we have said, copyright protects the expression of ideas, it is not confined to words, pictures or music as such. There is copyright in a compilation, such as a timetable. In the case of a book there is copyright not only in the text, but also separately in the typographical design of the book.

Ownership

The copyright of an original work is normally held by the author – the person who used his/her creative thought to produce it. There are, however, important exceptions. When work is produced in the course of employment, the copyright normally belongs to the employer, not the employee. (But although a newspaper proprietor has the right to use articles written by the staff in the newspaper, all other rights, such as the right to reprint them in book form, for instance, remain with the journalists who wrote them. This is a special case.)

A second exception, equally important for public relations people, is photography. Copyright in photographs that are *commissioned* is held by the person or company that commissioned them. You should, however, beware of one point in this regard. Even though you have commissioned a photograph, the negative remains the property of the photographer, unless you specifically arrange to buy it – so the photographer can make his/her own terms with you for supplying prints, though he/she has no right to supply prints to anyone else.

Copyright in a cinema film is owned by the maker of the film, and although this is defined as 'the person by whom the arrangements for the making of the film is undertaken', this is normally assumed to be the film company. When commissioning a film, it is usual to provide in the contract that the copyright shall be automatically assigned to the company or person that has commissioned it.

Copyright in television broadcasts (as distinct from the material they contain) is held by the BBC or the IBA as the case may be.

Although copyright of government documents and publications is held by the Crown, there is normally no objection made to reproducing parliamentary papers such as Bills, Acts, Statutory Rules and Orders, reports of Select Committees, or items in *Hansard* (the latter may not be used in advertising).

Performers' rights are a separate though related subject, and are now governed by the Dramatic and Musical Performers Protection Act 1958 and the Performers Protection Act 1963.

What copyright protects

Despite its name, copyright protects work not merely against being reproduced in any material form, but against such uses as translations, adaptations, or being performed or broadcast. It is sensible to assume, as a starting point, that you can make *no* use without permission of any work in which you do not own the copyright.

Nevertheless, there are certain practical exceptions. The law allows 'fair dealing' with a copyright work for research or private study or for criticism or review (provided there is proper acknowledgement), and in various other circumstances. Certain users by libraries are allowed, and also use for educational purposes. Records of musical works may be made under certain conditions where a fixed royalty is paid. Sound recordings of films or broadcasts may be made for private purposes.

How long does copyright protection last

In literary, dramatic and musical works copyright continues for the lifetime of the author of the work, plus fifty years from the end of the year in which he/she dies, but if the author dies before the work is published, the copyright runs for fifty years from the end of the year in which the work is first published (which may, of course, be a long time after his/her death, and then it may be difficult to discover the owner).

Copyright in artistic works, including photographs, continues for fifty years from the data of first publication, and the same thing applies to sound recordings and to films (except that with films other than newsreels, advertising films and some education films, the period runs from the date of registration).

No permission is needed to reproduce a work not published within one hundred years, and copyright in the typographical arrangement of a book lasts for twenty-five years.

International copyright

The Berne Convention of 1886 and the Universal Copyright Convention of 1952, which provide international copyright protection, require as a condition of that protection that published works bear the letter 'C' in a circle, accompanied by the name of the owner of the copyright and the year of first publication. Whether or not you have international circulation in mind, it is always a wise precaution to take this simple step.

Remedies for infringement

A plaintiff who proves that his/her copyright has been infringed can ask the court:

1 To grant an injunction to forbid any further infringement, temporarily (pending trial of the action) or permanently.
2 To award damages.
3 To order the defendant to render an account of the profits he/she has made through the infringement.
4 To order the infringing copies to be delivered up.

An action for infringement must be brought within six years of the act complained of. In some circumstances a breach of copyright law may be a criminal offence. Merely to possess a sound recording or film known to infringe copyright is, for instance, an offence.

Defences

Anyone sued for breach of copyright can claim in defence:

1 That there is no copyright in the work.
2 That the plaintiff is not the owner of the copyright.
3 That the material copied is not a substantial part of the work.
4 That the act complained of falls within the 'fair dealing' exceptions.

Registered designs

Copyright, although it arises automatically on the creation of a work, applies only if the work is 'original'. Certain types of design can be registered under the Registered Designs Act 1949. Registration is a kind of guarantee that the design *is* original: any infringement of a registered design is actionable, and it is no defence to say that the infringer thought up the same design independently. Moreoever, the mere fact of making known that the design is registered can put people on notice that the owner intends to protect it.

Registration is available only for designs intended to be reproduced in more than fifty articles, which is regarded as the criterion for 'industrial' designs; and sculpture, wall plaques and medals, and printed matter are excluded. Although the application to designs of industrial products in the ordinary sense is obvious, the method can be used for, say, a character created for advertising that could be exploited in or on forms such as T-shirts, toys, etc. Application for registration must be made before the design has been published (or publicly used) in any way. Protection for designs after 1 August 1989 is twenty-five years (provided the appropriate renewal fees are paid).

Copyright protection for products produced industrially and based on copyright drawings that are registrable is provided for a fifteen-year period.

Trademarks

Trademarks used in relation to goods can be registered under the Trade Marks Act 1938, and the Trade Marks Rules of the same year, with subsequent amendments.

A trademark need not of course be a symbol; it can be an invented word or words, some other word (but not one having a direct reference to the character or quality of the goods, or a geographical name or surname, though it can be the name of a company, individual or firm represented in some special way), or 'any other distinctive mark'. Protection lasts initially for seven years, renewable for periods of fourteen years.

Many trademarks cannot be protected under the law of copyright, or as registered designs. Trademarks registration fills the gap, though its limitation to use in relation to goods eliminates many 'corporate identity' symbols.

As a result of the Trade Marks (Amendment) Act 1984, it is now possible to register service marks, i.e. marks that identify services just as trademarks identify goods. Broadly similar rules apply to service marks as apply to trademarks.

Patents

Patents differ in kind from the other ways of protecting 'intellectual property' mentioned, in that they do protect workable *ideas* capable of industrial application, rather than the *expression* of ideas. The law is now largely set out in the Patents Act 1977. New inventions for which a patent is granted are protected initially for four years, and the period can be extended up to a maximum of twenty years (provided the annual renewal fees are paid).

International protection is available in one form or another for registered designs, trademarks, service marks, and patents.

All these forms of protection, like copyright, can be assigned complete, or licences may be granted by the holder to allow another party to use them for a period or in part. It will be seen that the different forms of protection may overlap.

Passing off

To pass off your goods or services as those of someone else is actionable. Recently the courts have tended to extend this protection to cover non-proprietary names such as 'champagne' (the only true champagne is that made in the Champagne area of France, and a French manufacturer successfully sued a Spanish firm that called its wine 'champagne'). It is fair to add that a name *can* become general property in time and lose this protection: Bath buns, for instance, can be made with impunity outside the City of Bath!

Passing off is often a possible alternative action to a claim for infringement of copyright: even if the copyright has not been infringed, a similar design or label could be held as 'passing off'. No actual damage need be proved, only a tendency to cause damage; and it is no defence to prove that the passing off was innocent or done without knowledge. Passing off could in appropriate circumstances also give rise to a criminal offence under the Trade Descriptions Act.

Breach of confidence

Misuse of ideas or information received in confidence from someone else can be the subject of an action for breach of confidence. In public relations this may apply to material received in confidence from a client or employer. It could also apply to a consultant's plan 'pirated' by some other person or company, though a claim on this basis would not succeed unless it could be shown that the ideas were original and not simply derived from common professional knowledge. It has even been suggested that if a house journal is supplied to newspaper editors on condition they do not publish certain marked stories, they could be sued for breach of confidence if they do so. In practice one feels public relations would not be helped by such a step!

Consumer protection law

This is now a large field, which the public relations practitioner will do well to read up in one of the specialist books on the subject. The relevant Acts are the Sale of Goods Act 1979, the Supply of Goods (Implied Terms) Act 1973, the Unfair Contract Terms Act 1977 and the Supply of Goods and Services Act 1982.

Another Act is the Trade Descriptions Act 1968, which makes it an offence to describe either goods or services inaccurately. It sets out the various points that must be correctly described, and the definition of 'trade description' is extremely wide: a description used 'in any manner likely to be taken as referring to the goods' could well cover, for instance, a press release or booklet.

The Food Act 1984 also makes it an offence to mislead on the nature, substance, or quality – including the nutritional value – of foodstuffs, and there are regulations made under this Act covering food hygiene and food labelling.

The Fair Trading Act 1973 set up the Office of Fair Trading, incidentally a valuable source of information on this whole field, and gave its Director General power to take legal action against manufacturers or traders who harm consumers. The Office encourages trade associations to produce voluntary codes of practice in their fields.

The Consumer Credit Act 1974 applies to all kinds of credit and hire transactions, mainly covering sums of £5000 or less. All businesses in this field now require a licence from the Director General of Fair Trading, and the Act and Regulations made under it require full information to be given in advertisements.

The Consumer Protection Act 1987 has tightened up the law on consumer safety and product liability. In addition, it has introduced new controls on misleading pricing supported by a comprehensive statutory code of practice.

Competitions

The organizing of competitions and related schemes is something that comes the way of most public relations practitioners at one time or another. Despite a number of exceptions, lotteries in general remain illegal in Britain. Any game of chance, in which people pay directly or indirectly to take part, may be held to be a lottery, and those who run it may be prosecuted under the Lotteries and Amusements Act 1976.

In a competition there must be sufficient skill in the competition to influence the result. Even a 'tie-breaker' has been held sufficient, if the first stage of the competition is so simple that no real skill is required to get the 'tie-breaker'. Fortunately there are exemptions for charitable and private lotteries, but unless you are certain that your scheme falls into a permitted category, it is sensible to make sure you are otherwise within the law.

The Act also forbids competitions in newspapers or magazines or in connection with trade, business or sale of any article to the public, in which prizes are offered for forecasting the results of events. Football pools do not come into this category, because they are regarded as a form of betting, and separately regulated.

Restrictive trade practices, monopolies and mergers, anti-competitive practices

Agreements or arrangements made between suppliers of goods or services which restrict competition have to be registered with the Director of Fair Trading. The law on this subject is now mainly to be found in the Restrictive Trade Practices Acts 1976 and 1977 and the Restrictive Practices Court Act 1976. The Treaty of Rome also contains provisions against agreements or arrangements that restrict competition, or restrict cross-frontier trade in the Common Market.

Monopolies and mergers are now covered by the Fair Trading Act 1973, and the Director General of Fair Trading has power to refer a monopoly situation to the Monopolies and Mergers Commission for investigation. Again, the EEC has rules against the 'abuse of dominant positions' that restrict competition. The Competition Act 1980 additionally controls what the Act terms 'anti-competitive practices'.

Professional discipline

The word 'profession' has two degrees of meaning in English. It is often used loosely as equivalent to 'occupation', as well as indicating a field of work with an advisory element whose practitioners are members of a professional body that requires them to have certain qualifications and to observe a code of professional conduct enforced by a disciplinary procedure. Public relations in Britain can claim to be a profession in this latter sense, though there is no legal or other requirement confining the practice of public relations to members of the professional body, the Institute of Public Relations.

The relationship of members to a professional body is an unusual one. If the association is (like the IPR) a company, the members of the association are the members of the company, and the members of the association's governing body are the directors of the company. But members are also bound contractually to the association. By their membership they agree to abide by the association's rules and to pay their subscription, in return for the rights of membership. If those rules require them to observe a code of conduct and to submit to penalties, including expulsion, and if they fail to do so, they have in such circumstances no legal claim against the association, for they have agreed to those rules. If the rules provide that decisions on disciplinary matters shall be announced publicly for the protection of the public, similarly they have no right of action, provided the announcement is not defamatory; and even if it is, it may be privileged.

This is one way in which a professional body can, under English law, maintain standards. Another is by protecting the right to claim membership of the association, or the use of letters indicating qualifications or membership. If a person uses the letters MIPR (Member of the Institute of Public Relations) or Dip.CAM (Diploma of CAM), for instance, without being entitled to do so, the body concerned can take action against him/her in the courts.

Conclusion

Clearly it has not been possible to do more in this chapter than give a bird's-eye view of some areas of the law of importance to the public relations practitioner. Although it is hoped that the introduction may be useful, do not rely upon it to find the definitive answer to a legal situation: space makes it impossible to give all the details and qualifications necessary, and the law is constantly developing.

A few practical words of advice with which to conclude:

1   Check and recheck any statement made in the course of your work, for accuracy and for its likely effect on those who receive it, looking for the worst interpretation that could be placed upon it.
2   When you are doing business, placing orders, or getting into any other contractual situation, get the full details clear and stated (or confirmed) in writing and accepted – preferably in writing – by the other party. For example, if you order a photograph or artwork, settle at the outset what rights you are buying.
3   Make sure you know a solicitor or other source of legal advice to whom you can turn for advice at short notice. It is worth establishing a continuing relationship and taking trouble to ensure that the solicitor knows what your work consists of for public relations practice is not always understood.
4   Save yourself time and money when you do consult a solicitor by marshalling all the facts and papers beforehand.
5   An ounce of care and commonsense at the time can save you the alternatives of conceding a claim, with consequent loss to you or your company, or having to oppose it legally at considerable cost.

13

International Public Relations

Sam Black

There is general agreement that 'international public relations' is very important, but here the agreement usually ends, for there is plenty of argument about what exactly is meant by this phrase.

By its definition as a management function, it is obvious that if an organization has interests outside its own geographical zone, its public relations activities cannot be restricted to the home market. I suggest that a working definition of international public relations postulates that it is 'the planned effort to establish mutual understanding by bridging a geographical, linguistic or cultural gap'. The problem may be related to one of these difficulties or to all three. This covers both instances where an overseas programme is planned or where home activities may have unexpected repercussions outside the country of origin.

By its nature, public relations policy can be decided centrally for implementation worldwide. When it comes to translating this policy into action, however, the programme that works very successfully in the home country may prove ineffective or even counter-productive overseas. Both the communication media and the acceptable style of messages are very local, even when different languages do not have to be used.

Even drawing up a simple news release may require a knowledge of local culture, religion, and traditional values if it is to ring true and not offend local susceptibilities. This aspect is even more important when planning a whole public relations programme or campaign.

Some of the large American corporations with widespread international operations tried at one time to organize and run all their public relations activities from the American headquarters. This was an abysmal failure and soon all these companies adopted the 'plan globally but act locally' policy.

Some inconsistencies

Some companies and some individuals appear to be hypnotized by the concept of 'international' public relations. An example of this is a true story told by Ellis Kopel. Some years ago his agency was asked to pitch for a public relations contract with the Cake and Biscuit Industries Trade Federation. The specification for the contract was the requirement to demonstrate an ability to work internationally. Kopel was able to show experience of working successfully internationally and won the contract. Having won the contract, Kopel held it for ten years, but at no time during that period was he called upon to do any work outside Britain.

Potential problems of linguistic differences

It is always necessary to watch out for ambiguity or *double entendre*. This can be difficult sometimes when using your own language but becomes a veritable minefield when it comes to composing messages in a foreign language. Even using the services of a national may not avoid problems unless they are familiar with the subject of the message.

A few examples will emphasize this point. A motor car did not sell in one country because its name when translated meant 'coffin'. An airline produced an advertisement publicising its 'rendezvous lounges' only to find out too late that in the local language it meant 'a place to have sex'. These are only two examples of the kind of embarrassing mistakes that can happen so easily when working overseas in an unfamiliar language.

Methods of organizing international public relations

The sad experience of American corporations was mirrored by that of other large companies endeavouring to carry out active public relations from far away in another continent. This led to the general adoption of four main methods of organizing public relations far from base:

1   There are a few public relations consultancies that can provide the services of their other subsidiaries in all the major industrial centres. The two best known examples of this are Hill & Knowlton and Burson-Marsteller.
2   Another choice is to employ the services of a group with fully or partly owned offices and affiliates worldwide. The leading example of such a network is Shandwick.
3   Several groups bring together independent public relations consultancies in the major industrial centres. Two well-known examples are the Pinnacle and Worldcom groups, which have members throughout the world.

4 Other networks operate on a very informal basis, even perhaps without regular meetings, and refer clients to each other and work together as appropriate.

The major difference between using these four different methods of securing support in different countries is the question of effective control. Control should always rest with the employer, but inevitably questions of choice that require immediate decisions may arise.

The influence of the International Public Relations Association (IPRA)

The formation of the International Public Relations Association in May 1955 led to a much better appreciation of how public relations practice operates in different countries.

Through its regular meetings and the Public Relations World Congresses held every three years, practitioners from over 60 countries have shared their knowledge and professional experience and this has undoubtedly raised the standard of competence worldwide. It has also made it possible for easy cross-border cooperation.

Since 1990, IPRA Golden World Awards for Excellence have recognized outstanding examples of public relations practice. Most of these winning case studies have been carried out in a single country but there have been a number of good examples of international public relations. The following are a few examples:

1 Texaco failed dismally in trying to secure permission to drill for oil off the Nova Scotia coast of Canada. Its high profile approach attracted so much adverse criticism that it gave up the attempt. Only a few years later a smaller oil company, LASMO, decided to have a try despite knowing all about Texaco's failure. The company, however, took local public relations advice and accepted the need to adopt a very low profile and to negotiate quietly with the fishermen and other interested parties before going public with their intentions. This excellent advice coupled with help in dealing with media relations led to a successful conclusion, and oil has been flowing out of the sea since 1992.
2 A high level industry initiative brought together a number of public and private organizations in the US to protect the global environment and to reduce damage to the ozone layer. A body, ICOLP, was formed, and major overseas bodies joined to make this effort truly international.

3 The benefits that can come from organ transplant are well-established
   but the work is handicapped by lack of sufficient donors. The European
   Donor Hospital Education Programme was set up with the objective of
   publicizing the problem across Europe. The case study described the way
   in which this objective was being achieved.
4 AT & T, the American communications giant, has employees all over the
   world, and one of its public relations objectives is to bring news about
   company activities regularly to all its workers. The target was to devise
   a scheme that would bring really important news to all employees before
   they read about it in the media. Taking advantage of the widespread
   availability and use of electronic equipment within the company, the
   company launched a daily electronic newsletter called *AT & T Today*. Its
   objectives were threefold:

   1 To provide timely information about the company and its competitors.
   2 To deliver important news immediately and cost-effectively.
   3 To create credible, candid two-way communication through a 'letters'
      section.

These four case histories illustrate a few different ways in which public
relations was used to support particular objectives. By their intrinsic nature,
public relations programmes or projects are likely to be as diverse as industry itself. Like any other management discipline, however, it is not an
isolated activity but supports and enhances the strategy and objectives of its
company or organization.

International media of communication

Using the media is one of the commonest means of communicating as a part
of a public relations programme. When working within your own country,
there is little difficulty in drawing up a suitable media list according to the
type of media it is planned to use. When it is desired to carry out media
relations at a distance, it may be difficult to prepare an appropriate media
list without local advice.

In such circumstances it is often decided to concentrate on the increasing
number of international business newspapers. The *Financial Times* now has
twenty-nine fully manned bureaux overseas, and international editions are
printed in the USA, Germany, France and Japan. The paper claims a circulation of over 100,000. The European edition of the *Wall Street Journal* is now
selling over 50,000, and also has an Asian edition selling about 40,000.
Another international newspaper circulating widely among businessmen is
the *International Herald Tribune*.

A new international medium that is becoming increasingly significant is the MBC satellite programme, which was founded in Saudi Arabia and broadcasts news, views and features to 100 million Arab viewers in the Middle East, Africa and Europe. It rivals in importance the BBC World Programme and CNN International.

In dealing with local and national media, local knowledge is essential, as the habits and methods of journalists and editors varies considerably from one country to another. When dealing with financial subjects internationally it is necessary to bear in mind the different time zones, which can·be very important when price sensitive subjects are being handled.

Speaking the right language

Even though we find today that computers can talk direct to other computers, this does not detract in any way from the importance of the spoken and the written word.

Within a country or a culture it is likely that words will mean the same thing, thus preventing misunderstandings. Unfortunately this is not universally true. It has been said that America and the United Kingdom are 'divided by a common language'. Although both countries use English as their national language, misunderstandings are common enough.

When working in an unfamiliar language, you must appreciate the potential differences between correct speech and the language as it is used colloquially. This danger dictates great caution in the choice of translators and interpreters.

Those of us who are not good linguists hail with satisfaction the increasing adoption of English as the common language of international public relations. This fact makes communication between countries easier but does not help when you are working inside a country where English is not well-known. There are many social advantages in being able to talk to people in their own language, but there are potential dangers in communicating or conducting negotiations without an experienced interpreter.

Non-verbal communication

There is another 'language' that can cause difficulties. Non-verbal communication, or body language as it is often referred to, can be used advantageously or can give serious offence.

There are four different types of actions which can be identified:

1　Symbolic gestures, such as a salute or thumbs up.
2　Emphasis while speaking, such as arms waving or pointing.

3   Facial movements of emotion, such as a smile, a grimace or a grin.
4   Nervous reactions, possibly indicating stress or nervousness, such as blinking, fidgeting or swaying backwards and forwards.

When controlled, these gestures can be used effectively to give emphasis to a speech or a delicate negotiation. When used unconsciously, or at wrong moments, they can prove counter-productive or even harmful.

Cultural differences

Apart from gestures and other body movements, there are many customs restricted to certain countries or races. These may relate to kinds of food, or how they are eaten, or to ways in which it is permissible to sit, or how to greet friends or strangers. Sometimes faults of etiquette may be laughed away, but at other times they may cause serious offence.

This field of human relations is a veritable minefield and it is necessary for those in public relations to be fully cognisant of these facts so that they can prevent their colleagues from giving involuntary offence.

Summing up

The four case histories that have been described above point to the problems that can arise when working beyond national frontiers but also the many opportunities for using imagination and creativity to prepare public relations programmes which can achieve ambitious objectives.

The theory and philosophy of public relations practice are similar whether the field of activity is at home or abroad. This means that the four stages of research – planning, implementation, monitoring and evaluation – apply equally. But immediately the detailed planning and budgeting starts, it is necessary to take into account the logistics and practical aspects peculiar to the territory where the programme will be implemented.

The axiom that it is possible to plan globally but action must be planned and implemented locally is the one feature of international public relations that cannot be denied. People trying to ignore this fact do so at their peril.

14

Crisis Management

Michael Regester

Each year companies invest large amounts of money and executive time in developing and maintaining their corporate reputations and those of their products and services. Few companies, however, have in place procedures and personnel who protect those reputations when a crisis occurs. This is in spite of the fact that there is much evidence to show that companies that have failed ·to communicate effectively during a time of crisis suffer sometimes irreparable damage to their reputations – damage which is readily measurable in bottom-line terms.

Some companies have paid the ultimate price for their failure to communicate in a crisis situation. Pan Am is such an example. It went bankrupt soon after Flight 103 exploded over Lockerbie.

On the question of the warning of a possible terrorist attack. Pan Am said at first that it was unaware of any warning, only to have it revealed later that all US carriers operating in Europe, including Pan Am, had been so informed. A cardinal principle of communicating in crisis situations had been breached. There simply are no secrets today. There are too many eager sources and too many persistent reporters. The key is to tell it all, tell it fast, and to tell it truthfully.

Generally, Pan Am's communications policy was not to communicate in the aftermath of the tragedy, on the grounds that the explosion was something 'that had been done to them'. It hadn't been caused by pilot error or engine failure, so why should the airline bother to comment?

The answer is that when a corporate tragedy occurs, people want to be *reassured*. They want to be reassured about three things:

1 That the company had everything in place to prevent the tragedy from occurring.

2   That, in spite of such preventative measures, the organization had the foresight to anticipate the possibility of something going wrong and knew what to do to solve the problem as quickly as possible.
3   That the organization cared about what happened; in other words, it was able to put a human face on the organization in its time of crisis.

Should those preventative measures prove not to have been in place, then the organization must demonstrate that significant changes are to be made to prevent such an event from occurring again.

In stark contrast to Pan Am, precisely such action was taken by Sir Michael Bishop, chairman of British Midland Airways, when one of his airline's Boeing 737s crashed at Kegworth, adjacent to the M1.

He raced to the scene of the accident, conducting 'live' radio interviews from his car 'phone as he travelled. When he arrived at the scene, he immediately gave live television interviews about what he was going to do and how he felt about what had happened. As a consequence, people did not lose confidence in the airline, or in Boeing 737s. When pilot error was found to be the cause of the accident, the pilot was fired.

But did Pan Am's CEO, Thomas Plaskett, appear? Apologise? Attend memoral services? Atone for irresponsibility? No he did not. Confidence in the airline evaporated. People chose to fly with other carriers. Pan Am went bust.

In today's age of corporate accountability companies must be prepared to communicate in a time of crisis. Preparation entails:

1   *Conducting a risk audit* – identifying areas where the company is most vulnerable.
2   *Identifying audiences* – who would demand information in a crisis situation and how would they be communicated with?
3   *Identifying and training spokespeople* – ensuring that members of senior management are trained in techniques for communicating with the broadcast and print media; and ensuring that teams of trained company personnel are available to deal with calls from customers and families of employees.
4   *Testing everything* – running simulations to test procedures and training programmes.

Ultimately, the objective of effective crisis communication planning is *to protect the business; perhaps even to save it.* If a company has a corporate soul, if it knows who it is, if it cares about what it does, it tends to communicate – and will survive the unthinkable. Anticipation and preparation are key to the ability to survive.

Conducting a risk audit

Companies will often claim that they have undertaken such an audit for insurance purposes – and of course, they have. But a 'risk' in the context of a crisis communications plan can vary considerably from a risk identified for insurance purposes.

My own definition of a crisis, in public relations terms, runs as follows:

> An event that causes the organization to become the subject of widespread, potentially unfavourable, attention from the media and other external groups such as shareholders, politicians, trades unionists and environmental pressure groups who, for one reason or another, have a vested interest in the actions of the organization.

By way of an example, a series of underground fires at a mine unknown to the local community would constitute a 'crisis' in the physical sense and cause grave consternation to the insurance men. It would not, however, constitute a 'crisis' within the definition for the purposes of this chapter.

When trying to identify potential crises in public relations terms, you may end up with a list that is two miles long, and when you present it to senior management, your credibility is lost. Potential crises therefore need to be prioritized, so that the list can be shortened to a manageable size. This is best achieved by applying the following criteria to the potential crises:

- Examine what crises have befallen the particular organization in the past, and those that have befallen similar organizations in the same industry/field before. If it has happened before, it can happen again.
- Look into the future. Do the organization's plans entail the prospect of an unfavourable reaction, e.g. causing large-scale redundancies, or commissioning new plant in a sensitive area? Is there new legislation being dreamt up in Brussels or Whitehall that could damage the organization's ability to continue operating? After all, as Dr Henry Kissinger once pointed out to Richard Nixon, 'an issue ignored is a crisis ensured'.
- Judge the impact that a particular crisis would have on audiences crucial to the organization and what an unsympathetic reaction from them would do to the bottom line. Could people be injured? Could the environment be harmed? What would happen to sales? Would the share price suffer?

An amalgam of the findings of this kind of research will produce a 'most likely' and 'most harmful' list of potential crises, which can then be planned for.

Identifying audiences

Whenever I am presented with a crisis situation, my first thought process is 'Who are the main audiences that need to be communicated with?' For example, when the company that owned the crude oil on board the tanker *Braer*, which smashed into rocks off the Shetland Islands in 1993, asked me to help, my first reaction was to think, mistakenly, that the media and the islanders themselves would form the principal audiences. Certainly, they were important audiences (more than 500 journalists from all over the world had flown to the Shetlands), but, as far as my client was concerned, its shareholders were by far the most important, immediate audience.

At the time of the *Braer* crisis everyone believed it was going to be a disaster of *Exxon Valdez* proportions. People who had followed the fortunes of Exxon, post-*Valdez*, knew that the company's bungling over communications had led to a boycott of Exxon products in the US and to many other measures that had contributed to a total bill to Exxon of some $7 billion! If my client's shareholders believed that their company was going to face a bill of similar size, what was going to happen to the share price? It was going to nosedive.

Our first step therefore was to obtain a suspension of dealing in the share price on the New York stock exchange until we could clarify to investors and their advisers the extent of the financial liability my client could face for oil clean-up and other associated costs. Once we had done this, and reassured shareholders that insurance policies were in place to cover these costs, the shares were listed again and dropped only 25 cents on the day's trading. After that, we could turn our attention to the media, the islanders, government departments and environmental groups, who formed the other key audiences in this situation.

It is virtually impossible to communicate with all key audiences at the same time during a crisis, so it is important to prioritize them, according to the particular situation, and then to decide what messages need to be communicated, by whom and how.

Identifying and training spokespeople

The crux of the bungled communication problem faced by Exxon during the *Valdez* disaster was the hopeless ineptitude of its chairman to act as a spokesman for the company during its time of crisis. This begs the question: should the chairman or CEO be the spokesman? Absolutely. Unless, of course he is incapable of presenting the company view in a manner that is perceived to be honest, forthright and sincere. Not all CEOs are capable of this and, in a major crisis, this is a serious handicap.

Training, before and during the crisis, can help enormously – not least because the process will help identify those within the company who possess a natural aptitude and those who do not. Such training, however, cannot be introduced after the crisis, though it can be reinforced at the time. James Burke, chairman of Johnson & Johnson, had such training before his national television appearances during the *Tylenol* crisis in Chicago.

Members of senior management need training in techniques for successfully handling television, radio and print media interviews, staging effective press conferences in what can be a hostile environment; and some organizations, depending on the nature of their business, may need back-up teams of telephone responders trained in techniques for responding to hundreds of calls from the media, relatives of employees and customers.

Most of the oil companies working offshore in the North Sea, and many of the public utility companies and airlines, have such back-up teams of responders, ready to swing into action at a moment's notice. (When the Piper Alpha tragedy struck in the North Sea, Occidental Oil had forty such responders trained in Aberdeen, and a further twenty trained at its London offices.)

One final question often posed with regard to spokespeople dealing with a crisis is 'Should the CEO always go to the scene?' Usually, the answer is 'yes', but it does not always follow. Sometimes the CEO can provide the proper responses from the home base. Going can, however, show care, compassion, and eagerness to correct the problem (as demonstrated by Sir Michael Bishop in the aftermath of the Kegworth crash).

The key is to show these characteristics; and, if it can be done more effectively from headquarters, fine. The chairman of *Exxon* felt that he could not leave his New York headquarters in the aftermath of the *Valdez* disaster. Perhaps he should have invited the press to come to him, and shared with them everything that was going on, especially during the first few days.

Testing everything

A survey recently conducted by my consultancy among *The Times* Top 1000 UK companies revealed that only 34 per cent of them had prepared crisis communications plans; of that 34 per cent, only 5 per cent had tested their plans! This is like saying 'Okay, we've developed the plans; let's see if they work when the crisis happens!'

Generally, that is not a good idea. Plans aways need fine-tuning and rehearsing to encompass changes in the organization's business, changes in attitude, and changes in personnel. Simulations to test such plans are today treated extremely seriously by a few companies – and valuable lessons are always learned from them.

The scenario for the simulation must be developed with great accuracy so that the whole exercise does not lose credibility when being enacted. Its contents, however, must remain privy to the developers and managers of the simulation.

Those expected to take part in the simulation should be warned that it is to take place during a particular month. But they should not be given the precise date or time, or of course any clue as to the nature of the problem that is going to arise.

Each simulation should be assigned a codename, which must be used as a prefix to any written or spoken words during the simulation so that if any information leaks out, it is not thought to be 'the real thing'. (This happened to me once when an over-zealous secretary in the public affairs department of the client company for which I was running the simulation faxed press releases to the real Press Association wire service instead of to the pretend one – with nearly dire consequences for the client concerned and my future relationship with them!)

It is also worth noting that external agencies, such as the police and fire services, will gladly take part in simulations because it enables them to test their response procedures as well.

My consultancy will often hire as many as eighty role-players to act out the parts of the media, customers, members of the public, politicians and others to put a client through its paces. The simulation should be immediately followed by a debrief, which takes account of any errors that have been committed and assigns responsibility for any necessary follow-up action.

Conclusion

In concluding this chapter, it is my belief that the successful management of the public relations aspects of emerging issues and actual crises represents the most valuable role which public relations practitioners can perform on behalf of their employers and/or clients. Communicating effectively during times of difficulty can, quite literally, save organizations millions of pounds and may save the business altogether.

The time and costs of the training and preparatory work of helping an organization to survive the worst of all possible circumstances is infinitesimal when compared to the cost of being unprepared.

15

Sponsorship

Margaret Nally

A good question could be 'Is sponsorship a tool or technique of public relations?' But it would be quite as good a question to ask whether it is a part of an advertising programme or marketing scheme.

The relationship between these three aspects of communication, as handled by CAM and subsequently by other sources of education and training, was not without problems. When CAM was established, there was considerable opposition to the concept that in the first stage of the courses each sector needed to learn about the others. Perhaps public relations people were the most anxious, probably because this was a comparatively new science, with less recognition and material backing and therefore tending to class itself in a defensive manner, as above the other operations.

This attitude was overcome and, as time progressed, without any denigration of publicity, advertising or professional marketing, it became generally recognized that public relations holds a wider brief, which can often mean that, in addition to its own mission or purpose, it is the coordinator of the interactive programme of a company, organization, group or person. Knowledge of the other areas has been accepted as not only in order but required.

As time progressed, too, the nature of sponsorship, what it means and achieves, has changed, and currently it is possibly the most obvious illustration of successful cooperation between those three aspects of communication.

A look back

In the years immediately after the Second World War, when public relations were developing in the UK and the USA, and moving into many other countries, sponsorship, even if not recognized by that name, was probably used more by public relations people than by advertising or marketing operators. This was because it was viewed as a type of patronage, support for good causes, which would enhance the reputation or image of the sponsor. There are many old tales of major organizations supporting favourite interests of the chairman or managing director, or their wives, with no real relevance to that organization's operation or purpose.

During the 1960s sponsorship began to be recognized as a useful, commercial part of advertising and marketing, mainly due to the development of television. Unlike the USA, where commercial support of programmes was, and still is, a routine matter, in the UK there were strict regulations affecting independent as well as BBC productions. These prevented promotion or mention of products or interests except within the advertisements shown by the commercial stations. Mainly in sport to start with, sponsorship was recognized as a means of getting a product or company name on to the television screen as an integral part of programmes in a way that could not be condemned by the authorities. See Figure 15.1.

An advantage of this era of sponsorship was that it introduced the reciprocal element, which had to be incorporated and much more developed

Figure 15.1 *Ernie Els (left) and Gary Nicklaus on the St Mellion course, taking part in the Benson & Hedges International Open Golf tournament. (Photo by Phil Shelton)*

later. Providing support via sponsorship was no longer to be a 'do good' gesture with possible recognition. It had to be a well-constructed, business cooperation, where the investment was to be matched by a suitable return.

By the advent of the 1970s it was not only being realized that the full value of sponsored operations could not be achieved without the assistance of linked public relations activity, but the importance of this tool as a method of communication in itself began to be exploited.

Further development

It has been said that sponsorship can reach widely different people who have one particular interest. It can also reach those same people in many countries, because it can overcome language problems.

The recognition of the influence of well-organized sponsorship, not only within television but in many other fields, encouraged the establishment of specialist agencies and their national and international associations. Thus initiating and 'marrying' links were formed between suitable programmes or recipients and the potential supporting agency, consultancy or organization.

The continuing introduction of new communication techniques, influencing as it does not only the national but also the international flow of news, comment, information and entertainment, increases the opportunity for sponsorship. Changes in legislation in the UK opened up new areas, especially in television. So, weather reports could be linked to an insurance company, a popular drama series featuring a fine-wine-drinking.barrister could be linked to the name of a port, though he could not be portrayed drinking that port. A series about a team of doctors, backed by a private health insurance plan, gained acceptance initially, but was then banned because the subject of the story was too close to the operation of the sponsor.

The actual placing of recognizable branded products within a TV scene is still not officially allowed, nor a mention on radio outside an advertisement slot, but in many TV and radio programmes, even BBC, particularly in the leisure and music areas, donated products or event tickets are used as prizes in competitions, thus achieving coverage.

There are also opportunities, especially with the increasing use of independent organizations to devise and produce both information and entertainment programmes and film for radio and television, specialist agencies dealing with product placement. This is not sponsorship as such but may be closely linked to it and, as with that activity, while it may be related to the advertising or marketing, it must also be within the public relations thinking and could be a part of that budget.

Music, theatre, book and some discussion programmes cannot avoid mentioning record companies, publishers, producers or creators, as this would be infringing copyright rules.

For and against

So, as there are continuing problems for sponsorship as well as expansion, there has come fresh debate about the character of the operation. Is the placing of nameboards around a football or cricket ground, a tennis court or a snooker table, and insignia on players' garments or logos on racing cars and drivers' helmets, advertising, marketing or public relations? Is the name of a product or company appearing at the beginning, end or in intervals of a TV programme, advertising, marketing or public relations? When the name of a grocery supermarket group always appears immediately under, and in the same box as, the daily recipe in a newspaper, what is this? There is no 'Advertisement Feature' note to be seen.

Newspapers, especially regional versions, and magazines are now happy to have special features and supplements financed. These will relate to some element that can link with or further the sponsor's interests while remaining under editorial control.

Banks and financial organizations may underwrite the business columns. Airlines, travel firms or leisure groups can support the holiday or travel pages. The Royal Mail has been known to ensure a good readers' letter section. Those already supporting a sport or a specific team can use encouragement of larger sport sections to supplement the impact of their basic programme. Many organizations sponsor theatre, music and the arts, with this acknowledged in programmes, catalogues and advertisements; so, it is in their interest to ensure that publications can provide ample space for critical coverage and reporting.

It has to be appreciated that, just as with the television and radio programmes, the content of the sponsored item or section has to be editor-independent and unbiased. Once the copy is prepared or dictated by those subsidizing the published item, it becomes an advertising feature or advertorial, and has to be clearly identified as such. However, this does not exempt it from the attention of the public relations thinking. Good advertorials need the editorial media treatment of public relations, need to be coordinated within the general programme, and can be regarded as an allied element of sponsorship activity.

Matched marriages

It has already been established that sponsorship, like other areas of communication, has to be carefully organized and capable of proving its worth to public relations, i.e. results and value against the investment. There are additional aspects for this sector, such as consideration of complete suitability and matching of the support with the recipient; also consideration of the time scale of the operation with the capability of the support. There have been sad examples of lack of attention to such matters.

The first London Marathon, developed to be the largest in the world, was sponsored by Mars, the confectionery product well-known by its promotion as a source of energy. It was thus very appropriate and able to maximize on the investment. The second sponsor, which took over after Mars at the conclusion of the previously arranged term, was a financial, umbrella organization virtually unknown to the general public and certainly not connected with sport, energy or stamina. In spite of expensive television advertising in an attempt to get the name known, it is unlikely that this exercise was less than that of a totally negative return.

A textile company, as part of its promotional launch programme for a new fabric announced its sponsorship of three aspiring designers on their three-year course, which would include study of the use of the material. Unfortunately the fabric was a market failure and the company, not having taken this possibility into account, had to cancel the scheme abruptly, and the three students had to leave college without the qualifications they were seeking.

Negotiation changes

Both an advantage and an added concern in dealing with the area is that now most sports organizations, theatre companies, museums and galleries, even charities, have their own business managers or departments. These operate professionally in seeking support and ensuring that arrangements are based upon sound, businesslike, mutually advantageous precepts.

Some observers suggest that, with the increased professionalism now operating, the role of the specialist agency will decrease. There will be more direct negotiation between the sponsor and the subject, which will include all the ancillary action to support and exploit the programme for both sides.

There is also the feeling that certain aspects have been overworked or that there are too many sponsors trying to invest in the same area or in the same way. This is probably true of some sports and thus there is a need for imaginative thinking, as well as everything else, and new areas of operation are being investigated.

Legislation and social trends are influencing this field as much as general public relations and other forms of communication. Growing disapproval of tobacco, alcohol and dangerous activities has to be taken into account and may lead to further legislation. On the opposite balance, increasing awareness of, interest in and responsibility for environmental matters, as well as social and cultural themes, are opening up fresh and important opportunities and demands.

Ongoing potential

With this scenario it is possible to review the contribution sponsorship can make it a public relations programme and, equally, what public relations can contribute to a sponsorship arrangement. As a start one can look at the basic list of areas of public relations operation: financial, consumer, business to business, community, charity, staff and internal, local and national government, and corporate. Of course it is usually said that the last may be influenced by all the others, and an international element will come in where the subject is operating in more than one country.

In every one of these areas there are to be seen examples of the use of sponsorship, and even more opportunities can be devised with an intelligent, imaginative approach. It can start as a marketing tool, an advertising ploy or corporate promotion, but public relations will have to come in and can build upon it. This goes back to that cooperation, cross-fertilization, which sponsorship both needs and encourages.

In the financial area many leading banks choose to support music, theatre and art. An obvious link here is that the people interested in classical music, good theatre, sculpture and pictures are likely to be the best customers of a bank: visitors from other countries are also likely to be of a similar type, possibly engaged in business and finance at home.

The hosting of visiting cultural interests, such as music, dance and exhibitions, is also useful in the cultivation and maintenance of international banking business. Midland Bank has invested in many such concepts and continues to do so. With its supports of music and opera it makes use of its familiar promotional slogan, 'The listening bank'.

Other banks, such as Lloyds, support competitions and scholarships for young musicians, artists, actors and writers, with the consideration that they will be enlisting the interest of parents, relatives and associates, and also cultivating future customers.

Banks in other countries, such as Spain, Norway, China and Japan, have sponsored the visits of their native artistes and collections to centres abroad. If not useful in encouraging actual financial business for themselves, this can stimulate the right type of tourist business, thus improving commerce in general.

Obviously the additional element in the choice of subjects for support is the contribution to the corporate image and reputation achieved.

The major part of the sponsorship by UK banks emanates from their public relations departments. Visiting organizations require the same support and communication and will frequently rely on local practitioners.

Much of the other sponsorship in the financial area can also fall into the business to business bracket. It usually comprises top-level, discreet award schemes, and debates and conferences aimed at the various sectors of the field with which co-operation is required.

The cross-fertilization previously referred to comes in again and again. Where sponsorship in itself may not seem to be very much a part of business to business public relations, the programmes established to assist other areas, whether consumer, corporate or finance, can be employed to extra advantage here. Events or occasions of any type provide the opportunity for selective entertainment and hospitality for business contacts.

To summarize, although referring to the financial sector here, any well-constructed sponsorship operation can be utilized to contribute to several areas of a public relations programme, whatever its prime base. In addition, the scope is extending.

If, as is suggested, the sports area may be overcrowded, and some others, such as exhibitions, awards and special events or publications, may be overworked, there is no need to reject the possibility of a fresh approach. In addition, there is the whole area of global environmental and social conscience, which has already become not only one that will be seeking more and more investment, but at the same time opens new avenues for good activity on behalf of most aspects of a public relations plan.

Implementation

Returning to the matter of that planning required, it cannot be over-emphasized that a forecast of the time scale is essential. The organization and planning of the subject, even people's jobs, depend upon an arranged period of support. In most cases there is also a review period under which the sponsor will have agreed to assess the operation and give notice of whether it is intended to conclude at the time originally agreed, or whether a further extension of support is on offer. So, the subject will know what to do. It can either accept the further support or not, or take action to organize other arrangements.

One example of a long-standing, renewed sponsorship is the classic case of Cornhill and Test cricket. This is classic in the consumer area, as well as regards the financial and corporate aspects.

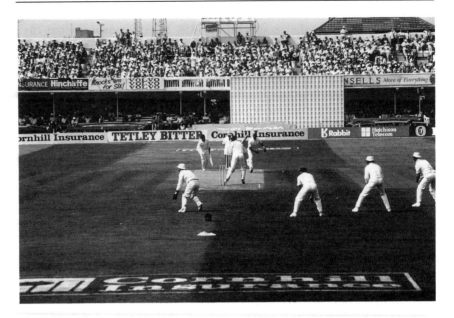

Figure 15.2   *A crowd of cricket lovers watch a Cornhill Test Match, England versus the West Indies, at Trent Bridge, Nottingham. Television viewers see the name on the pitch as well as on the boards (Photo by Patrick Eager)*

It is classic in the subject chosen and in the carefully measured results. When what was then a comparatively small company decided to allocate the whole of its promotional budget to the support of Test cricket, public knowledge of the name was minimal and it was virtually unconnected with insurance.

This was an occasion when the personal interests of the senior executive were a felicitous match to the interests of the organization. Linking with a sport that has the characteristics of 'truly English', 'fair play' and 'establishment' could not be more appropriate for an insurance company. See Figure 15.2.

Then, a vast proportion of the public interested in cricket and following the play would be just the types likely to be persuaded of the value of insurance. So, as the research has shown, the company name has become well-known and synonymous with insurance, and the business has prospered. A good reward for daring to save Test cricket!

There are other examples of multi-effective and long-running operations, and although these can come from large, major organizations, the basic thinking can be adapted for more modest investment.

Tangent effect

The Coca-Cola Company has the reputation of having its name signs everywhere in the world, including the most remote swamps and deserts. It is also classed as the biggest sponsor in the world. Over the years many types of programme have been used, some quite blatantly marketing- and selling-based. Major sport events have been used with a contract that ensured the product was the only soft drink promoted and on sale.

Then, as a result of the contact with the international football federation in the negotiations for major matches, and bearing in mind the vast children and young people market, the concept of sponsoring a scheme to introduce the game and train young players in undeveloped countries was born.

The resulting operation was a great success and has continued. The public relations people have confessed that they did not appreciate to start with just what a valuable tool it was to be. It is reported as benefiting the corporate and social image in each country as well as internationally, and has also aroused staff interest and loyalty.

Cultivating the interest of young people is not limited to organizations whose major market is, like Coca-Cola and McDonald, in that area. As already said, the banks aim to contact them with their general sponsorship and also use special programmes for schools.

Another long-standing project, which has become established on a global basis, is the 'Whitbread' – the name by which the four-yearly, round-the-world yacht race is called, with many local pronunciations. It may be difficult to appreciate what value such an enterprise could be to an organization mainly producing English beer and running English public houses. A full-time, permanent staff in the UK has been set up, with part-time representatives in all ports of call and a crowd of additional staff during the months of the race.

Apart from achieving such wide familiarity for the name, with vast, comprehensive media coverage, it has given the company healthy status in the corporate and financial fields. It has provided ammunition for public relations programmes backing the development and marketing of established activities, and also for new ventures in food and leisure both in the UK and overseas. Here it has been especially useful in assisting internal relations, ensuring support from the different types of staff newly recruited for fresh areas.

Into education

On the young people front the 'Whitbread' is ideal for adaptation. Many a geography class charts the movement and progress of the yachts on a large

Figure 15.3 *Children at an Exmouth primary school display the names of the yachts in the Whitbread Round-the-World race, which they have adopted and whose progress they follow from start to finish*

map throughout the race, accompanied by general information on climate and other aspects of the locality of each stage. Videos of the scenes add to the interest. See Figure 15.3.

It has to be noted that when sponsoring material for schools and other educational establishments, care has to be taken to ensure that it is genuinely useful information – straightforward communication on the subject. In other words, it has to be good public relations. Publicity or promotion are not acceptable.

This does not mean that the source of the material cannot be obvious to the students, teachers and relatives – it is a case of linked interest. Some programmes include inter-school or student competitions, which increase the reward potential.

In the cases of support for university study the benefit may be the linking of the organization's name with the title of the course or the resulting award or achievement. The investment may include, in addition to subsidy, a first job agreement for the student.

A trend in education that has now moved down from the higher levels to even the junior schools is that of setting investigative projects. Especially with the younger pupils, these incorporate the other trend of parent participation. Even with quite a modest budget, sponsorship of material for use by pupils or students on this work could be achieved as part of local or national public relations. Of course the information provided would relate to the background or interests of the sponsor.

Name recognition

While still on the younger generation, there are two more examples, perhaps classic, of the intermix of public relations with other routes of communication.

Pears Transparent soap was first marketed by a family firm of that name more than 200 years ago, and original, innovative ideas were used in the advertising to promote sales. One of these was the purchase in 1876 of Millais' painting 'Bubbles', which became a mainstay of the Pears image. In 1958, when the original company had become part of an international group and selling was in a much more competitive field, the Miss Pears annual contest was conceived as an extension of the 'preparing to be a beautiful lady' advertising campaign. A national competition, with regional preliminaries, this has become a top media event, locally, nationally, even internationally.

Is it sponsorship? It certainly has all the elements of such in its format, and also many up-and-coming artists have benefited, as, since 1968, a portrait of the winning young lady has been commissioned, retaining that early Pears connection with art and supporting the artist. The operation, which has ensured continuation of the brand name and reputation, has been handled by a public relations company, which has won awards for it work.

The second example is the established, long-recognized drink for Wimbledon tennis players – Robinsons Barley Water. It was probably a move that could be called public relations or even product placement now, but not back then in 1934 when it started. With the advent of TV coverage and clever exploitation in advertising, what could have become a passé beverage has retained its name and cachet. Although the Lawn Tennis Association has never allowed the name of the product to be directly linked with the event, the value of the investment has been well achieved.

Both these examples bring in the name, not of the company, but the brand of the product. There is an increasing importance being placed in corporate and financial affairs upon the value of an established, recognized name. In mergers and take-overs the value of a brand name is part of the commercial consideration. Public relations consideration of the use of sponsorship may therefore have to give more thought to achieving actual name recognition and approval as part of the corporate and financial activity.

Large and small

An interesting source of public relations use of sponsorship has been Japan, where organizations have needed to prove they are not a lot of new, upstart operations that have materialized only after the Second World War. Many companies have been able to link themselves with long-established sports events, and top level cultural and environmental projects. It has been possible, using these programmes, to illustrate past history and/or forward thinking.

By supporting one of the oldest sporting events – the Davis Cup, established in 1900 – Nippon Electric Co. Ltd, NEC, was able not only to further establish its name in hi-tech, modern activities but also emphasize its pedigree as a company founded in 1899.

Another more recent example was the no-expense spared investment by Nippon Television in the restoration of the Sistine Chapel in Vatican City. Although there has been controversy between experts on the methods used, the work has been declared the most important art restoration project of the twentieth century.

Apart from its widely recorded connection with this cultural and environmental success, Nippon Television took care to invest even more money in filming and documenting the process throughout its fifteen years. In return, it has sole rights to reproduction of the restored paintings for a specified period. This will no doubt be utilized to expand public relations and business activity.

It may seem a little ridiculous in comparison but many businesses and companies gain a good public relations return from the support of quite small events and institutions. Even in London and other large cities the careful choice of a sponsorship subject can enlist goodwill, both business and social, promote staff relations and encourage media coverage. In a more local situation the return can be even more relevant. Most small exhibitions, competitions, museums and events, that contribute to community life rely upon sponsorship. With proper handling, such support can add to the public relations effort as well as to general promotion.

One on one

Another aspect of sponsorship is where smaller schemes are linked to a larger one. Two of the major operations already mentioned illustrate this type of piggy-back connection.

Each of the yachts taking part in the Whitbread need to obtain sponsorship in order to cover the cost of the voyage. Not only is there the provision and maintenance of the boat, with its special equipment, to be covered, but also all the special provisions, clothing and other survival items for the crew. Many supply organizations use sponsorship within an event of this type as a means of both testing specialized products and creating material for subsequent public relations work.

Yachts accepted for the race can be sure of the media cover organized by Whitbread, especially television, much of which is also sponsored. This assists in the recognition of the more visual elements of sponsorship, but each participant will also rely on the benefit of being connected with a famous event to achieve wider return.

With the London Marathon the linking is of a different nature. Here, with the publicity accorded to the event, plus the challenge it offers, many organizations, especially charities, utilize it to obtain sponsorship of entrants to raise funds. Other participants may be used to arouse interest in promotions or campaigns – in fact for public relations – again using the connection with the established event.

Returning to the smaller budget scene, the same concept can apply. There are many regional and local events and programmes that offer opportunities for useful investment, especially in the community and environment areas. It has been known for a store to provide rubbish bins in a shopping precinct. Is this public relations or promotion? Whatever it is, it is sponsoring social and health programmes.

Where now

As already stated, the expansion of the technology of communication is adding to the abilities and responsibilities of public relations. There is the growth of more specialized and regional provision both by radio and television, matching, perhaps superseding, the printed media, with similar opportunities for sponsorship. Even more, the increasingly international scope of television will certainly lead to the creation of further major events and presentations, as well as providing more opportunity for sponsorship of general programmes and videos.

All the new projects are likely to include moves into the growing areas of both national and international interest, environment, community and social considerations. Both in themselves, and any back-on concepts, all will need the support of public relations and, at the same time, provide opportunities for imaginative, strategic public relations thinking.

In spite of any debate, and whether sponsorship becomes a more or less separate entity, there is no doubt that it will continue to be a useful part of public relations – both as a means and as a customer.

16

Education, training and career prospects

Sam Black

Public relations is still a second career for many entrants to the profession but it is now possible to study public relations in the United Kingdom at college or university – full-time, part-time or by distance learning.

In earlier years public relations practice mainly attracted journalists. Some barristers, civil servants, economists, or those working in marketing or general management were also attracted by the opportunities in this new profession. These men and women brought with them many skills and talents but they had to learn the specific requirements of everyday practice. While it is likely that some people will continue to move across from other fields, there are now excellent opportunities for studying public relations in depth at both the postgraduate and undergraduate levels.

From its formation in 1948, the Institute of Public Relations has paid considerable attention to training and education, both for practitioners and for potential entrants to the field. The IPR held seminars and conferences for its members and introduced a programme of certificate and diploma examinations for those wishing to qualify in this new profession.

In 1970 the Institute joined with other bodies to form the Communication, Advertising and Marketing Education Foundation (CAM), to run joint examinations to replace those which had been offered separately by the IPRA and the other associations.

The CAM Certificate Examination covers six subjects: Public Relations, Marketing, Advertising, Media, Sales Promotion and Direct Marketing, and Research and Behavioural Studies. Each subject has a three-hour examination and it is necessary to pass all six subjects to gain the CAM Certificate. Having gained the CAM Certificate, candidates can study for the Public Relations Diploma, which requires passes in three subjects: Public Relations Management, Public Relations Practice and Management and Strategy.

Courses preparing for the CAM examinations are held at public and private colleges throughout Britain. Over 1000 students register with CAM each year. Fewer than 4 per cent are full-time students. Most are working in public relations or allied fields. The majority of CAM students are aged between twenty-five and thirty and nearly 50 per cent are graduates.

It is necessary for prospective students to register with CAM before commencing their studies and full details are available from The CAM Foundation, Abford House, 15 Wilton Road, London SW1V 1NJ. Telephone: 0171-828 7506.

The CAM Diploma in Public Relations is one of the qualifications accepted by the Institute of Public Relations as eligibility for full membership. Evidence of four years' comprehensive experience is also required. This requirement of a recognized degree or diploma was introduced by the IPRA in January 1992. In considering applications from colleges for recognition of their courses, the Institute looks at the number of contact hours and their coverage of all the subjects detailed in the Public Relations Matrix developed by the Public Relations Education Trust (PRET).

The London Chamber of Commerce and Industry examines for the Diploma of Management Principles. This includes, at the Third Level, examinations in public relations at the certificate and diploma levels. These qualifications are accepted by some British universities as meeting their entry requirements. For information, contact The London Chamber of Commerce and Industry Examinations Board, Marlowe House, Station Road, Sidcup, Kent DA15 7BJ. Telephone: 0181-302 0261. LCII diplomas are accepted by CAM for certain exemptions from the CAM Certificate examination. Consult CAM Foundation or London Chamber of Commerce and Industry Examinations Board for details.

University programmes in the United Kingdom

Since 1987 university colleges have begun to offer public relations programmes. The breakthrough came with the validation of the one-year full-time postgraduate masters course at the University of Stirling, leading to a MSc degree. This multi-disciplinary programme lasts one year and includes the requirement of a dissertation. In 1991 a three-year distance-learning version of the MSc programme was introduced successfully.

A rather similar one-year full-time masters programme is available at Manchester Metropolitan University, leading to an MA in Public Relations.

An MA in European Public Relations can be taken at the College of St Mark and St John, Plymouth. This was introduced at the initiative of the European Public Relations Confederation and is a joint programme in

England, Belgium, France, Germany, The Netherlands and Portugal. The degree is validated by the University of Exeter and the Sorbonne.

A postgraduate diploma course in international public relations was sponsored by the Public Relations Consultants Association (PRCA), and the one-year full-time programme has been running successfully at West Herts College, Watford Campus, since 1987. The course includes a compulsory second language, French or German, and during the year there are joint meetings with students from a Paris college. The syllabus is both theoretical and professional.

At the undergraduate level there is now a wide choice of courses leading to a bachelor's degree. In 1994 the Institute of Public Relations recognized six undergraduate degree programmes in addition to the CAM Diploma and the three postgraduate courses described above.

The 1994 approved undergraduate degree courses are BA Hons in Public Relations at Bournmouth University; Diploma in Public Relations at College of Rathmines, Dublin; BA in Communication at Napier University, Edinburgh; BA Hons in Public Relations at Leeds Metropolitan University; Combined Honours Degree in Public Relations, University of Central Lancashire; and BA Hons in Public Relations at College of St Mark and St John, Plymouth (Exeter University).

This list is likely to increase as new degree programmes apply for recognition. Full details are available from the Institute of Public Relations (IPRA). The Old Trading House, 15 Northburgh Street, London, EC1V 0PR. Telephone: 0171-253 5151. All the university and CAM courses emphasize the importance of securing practical experience as well as academic qualification, and the programmes include opportunity for placements for a short or extended period.

Postgraduate degree programmes in public relations are being planned at several British universities. Bournemouth University, London Guildhall University and Leeds University have announced their intentions in this respect.

Public relations content in management studies

Since public relations is a management discipline, it is logical that an understanding of public relations should be part of all management education. MBA and similar programmes usually include marketing as a core subject, but public relations is seldom included even as an elective. This situation is now improving and many business schools now teach public affairs or public relations as part of their syllabus. The same is now true of management and business studies at different levels in many UK colleges.

Professional development

In common with people working in other professions, public relations practitioners are expected to continue their training throughout their professional career. The IPRA and the PRCA both organize seminar programmes each year and many other courses are available from public and private colleges and organizers. In addition, professional conferences are organized regularly by the Institute of Public Relations, the European Public Relations Confederation (CERP), and the International Public Relations Association (IPRA). These events provide opportunities for the discussion of new theories and techniques and the report on research projects.

The Institute of Public Relations is considering the introduction of a continuing development programme for all its members.

Qualities required for success

Since public relations practice encompasses such a wide field, with many different types of activity, there is no single list of ideal qualifications.

The basic requirements are commonsense and curiosity, combined with a mastery of spoken and written language. Other qualities required are those needed for any important and demanding occupation, such as flexibility and a capacity for hard work. Ideas and creativity are very important but it has been said with some truth that 'public relations is 10 per cent inspiration and 90 per cent perspiration'. Only students with a strong motivation to communicate and to deal with people are likely to succeed.

'Liking people' is not a significant attribute. It is helpful to 'like' all the people with whom one comes into contact but so far as our work is concerned it is much more important to be 'interested' in people and to understand how they form opinions and develop attitudes.

It is important for public relations practitioners to have a wide knowledge of current affairs and to know where to go for specialized information of all kinds.

The Public Relations Education Trust (PRET), which is jointly administered by the IPR and PRCA, has developed a matrix for public relations education and training. This matrix, which is updated regularly, describes the various elements of knowledge and skill required at each of five career stages.

Career prospects

Surveys carried out regularly by the Institute of Public Relations show that fully experienced practitioners can expect to receive remuneration in keeping with the rewards of similar professions. Public relations cannot be recommended, however, as a career for those who regard high financial reward as their chief goal. Like working in other professional spheres, there is a considerable sense of personal achievement and there are very good financial rewards for those who reach the top of the tree. This applies equally to those working in-house or in large or small consultancies.

There are equal opportunities for both men and women, and it is noticeable that many women are now holding very senior positions in public relations. All the largest national and regional public relations associations have had women presidents or chief executives in recent years. A relevant statistic is that in the International Public Relations Association, where membership is restricted to senior practitioners with at least five years' experience at a senior level, the proportion of women members has been rising steadily, and in 1993 was 28.72 per cent.

Index